So, you want to join the gig economy... now what?

Tales From a Freelance Veteran

ISBN 978-1-7946-0665-4

Jacket and book design by Eric Hartke

First edition

For my clients, who made every lesson in this book possible.

I am motivated every day by your trust in the Hartke Designs team, your humanity, and our collaboration.

Contents

Chapter One

First Things First:

Gig Economy 101

You might be wondering... What exactly is the gig economy? According to the Cambridge English Dictionary, a gig economy "is a way of working that is based on people having temporary jobs or doing separate pieces of work, each paid separately, rather than working for an employer."

It's also sometimes referred to as the sharing economy, collaborative economy, platform economy, networked economy, and the on-demand economy. And, by the time you are reading this book, there will likely be a few other names as well. The linguistic fuzziness might imply that this is a new phenomenon. But to people like me, this is how we've been working for years. And, if you picked up this book, you are likely considering joining the ranks of the gig economy. Awesome! You have an exciting road ahead. And many, many things to consider.

If you decide to make the leap, it might be useful to understand all the ways you or others might refer to your employment status. The workers who populate the gig economy are referred to as many things. Here's a list of what I've seen over the last decade:

- Freelancer
- Entrepreneur
- Solopreneur
- Free agent
- Giger
- Contractor
- Contingent worker
- Consultant
- Nontraditional worker
- Independent

- Independent worker
- Independent earner
- Digital nomad

If you consider yourself any of these things, it means you choose the projects you work on, money comes in from multiple sources, and you have a short-term relationship with your clients (although, that is not necessarily the case—more on that later). For the purposes of this book, I'll refer to those of us who work in the gig economy interchangeably as "independents" and "consultants." And, I'll refer to the people who hire us as "clients" and "customers."

Who makes up the gig economy?

It's also helpful to break the workers in the gig economy into categories— because as with any workforce, we're not all the same. We have different motives, goals, and aspirations for our independent lifestyles. The McKinsey Global Institute identified four categories in their 2016 report, Independent work: Choice, necessity, and the gig economy.

A **free agent** is a person who considers themselves a full-time independent and earns their primary income from independent work. They might be a self-employed electrician, a therapist with a private practice, or a web designer for hire. These people typically decide to "hang out a shingle," leave their full-time jobs, and don't look back.

A **casual earner** uses independent work to augment their primary income—moonlighters or people with a side hustle. They might be a graphic designer who creates logos on the side, a hobby photographer who sells their photographs, a person who puts their home on Airbnb when they are out of town on vacation or business trips. These people typically make enough money in their primary employment, but either because of a passion or a targeted need—like saving for a family vacation or buying a car for a new driver in the family—they pick up jobs on the side.

A **reluctant** is a person who earns their primary income from independent work, but would prefer a traditional full-time job internal to an organization. They might be someone who was laid off and is filling the gap while they job search or someone making a career transition who is picking up work in their former field while they lay the groundwork for the next career.

The **financially strapped** are those people who do independent work to augment their income to make ends meet, but would prefer not to do so. They might be an office assistant who bartends on the weekends, a teacher who tutors after school, or a mechanic who drives for Lyft after the kids go to bed.

There are tips and tricks in the following pages that will help anyone from any of these categories. Let's face it, no matter where you fall, you'll need to understand how to manage your independent income. You'll need to consider how you are going to find customers. And, once you have your customers, you'll need to understand what goes into a solid agreement or contract, and then you'll need to actually fulfill on the work.

If you are a **free agent** standing on the precipice and are considering making the leap into the gig economy, this book gives you a roadmap to get there. As a fellow free agent who made the leap in 2009, I offer my own experience and hard-won wisdom. I'll share the good, the bad, and the ugly—because as with any path we take in life, working in the gig economy has it all.

And for you **reluctants** out there who may have gotten shoved out onto the precipice... I am glad you picked up this book! My little secret is that I am a reluctant hiding in a free-agents' clothing. Let me tell you a little about my journey...

A reluctant free-agent

I started my career as a 23-year-old middle school teacher in central Indiana. And, I'm not going to sugar coat it—there was no way being a teacher was going to give me the financial security and lifestyle I imagined. I grossed $16,000 my first year and worked as a lifeguard and swimming instructor on weekends and in the summer—and not because I loved lifeguarding. While I was not an independent worker, I was *for sure* financially strapped! Had Lyft been around in 1997, I'm pretty sure I would have been driving for them.

I went back to graduate school (where I borrowed another $28,000 on top of the $30,000 I owed from my undergrad degree) and got my Masters in Instructional Systems Technology. And, although I didn't know it at the time, that decision to go back to school put me on a crash course with the gig economy.

After graduate school, I went to work in the performance development department (aka, learning and development) at the Walgreen Co. I had superb and highly supportive bosses and the company from the C-suite on down provided an outstanding place for a farm kid from Southern Indiana to cut her corporate teeth. While there, I worked on highly strategic initiatives in the pharmacy, beauty, and front-end areas of the stores that helped plant the seeds for the consultant I was to become.

It was also during this time that I began attending local chapter events of the learning industry's professional associations in Chicago. At these events, I began building my network. I mention this because I can trace 85% of my current business relationships to the three years spent at Walgreens and the network I started building during that time.

But, not one to let the grass grow under my feet, I left Walgreens and went to work for Type A Learning Agency, a boutique learning company in Chicago. It was at Type A where I learned the ins and outs of client service, project management, and how to accurately scope a project. Like my time at Walgreens, I was blessed by the Universe to work for an exceptional boss and alongside a wonderfully talented and creative team. I also got bit by the professional services bug.

Wow, did I ever discover that I loved... I MEAN LOVED... navigating in and out of different organizations across a variety of industries. I had a blast crisscrossing the country helping clients dig into their human performance issues and finding the solutions that were going to make a difference to the people working in these companies and to the bottom line.

But, they say timing is everything... and the boom-to-bust nature of the 2000s supports that notion. I joined Type A in early 2005 and, sadly, this creative little company didn't make it through the 2008 financial crisis. This is where my conundrum of identifying as a reluctant versus a free agent comes in. I wish I'd been financially tuned in enough at the time to make connections between the chaos boiling up on Wall Street and the decline in Type A's book of business—yeah, I know, "Duh!" All I knew was that there was a lot of stress and pressure to find new projects, and well, not many were landing.

Since my earliest days, I've tried to avoid stress or pressure and have always been instinctually aware of negative energy—quickly retreating to the quiet of the basement when adult conversations were happening in my childhood home. So, while I wasn't completely aware of *why* things weren't working, I was tuned in to the fact that they weren't working.

My gut told me to start looking at my options. I considered searching for a full-time position, but there was not a lot that sparked my interest out there (see aforementioned financial crisis). I also considered taking on a sales role at Type A. But, that did not align with how I saw myself or what I considered was my skill set at the time. So, that left one avenue...become an independent.

Until this point in my career, I'd never even considered this path. My personal narrative at the time was, "I'm social. I like people. I can't imagine being alone all day." And, while I knew I could fulfill on any work that came my way, I was not certain that work *would* come my way—and I hated selling, so figured I'd never be able to find my own projects.

Simply said, I was nervous and not entirely convinced I could make the independent life work. I did a lot of deep thinking and talked with trusted advisors—which I'll share more about in the pages to come. And then the Universe stepped in and gave me a sign. The owner closed the office and the whole team started working remotely. This move, from my perspective, was the beginning of the end. I began to plan my exit strategy and Hartke Designs was born.

As I reflect back, it strikes me as funny that leaving full-time employment felt more stable to me than staying, but staying inside a company where there was so much stress and pressure felt more unstable to me than setting out on my own. And, as it turned out, my belief in myself, the trust from my clients, and my trust in the fellow sub-contractors I've hired over the years has paid off.

I grossed $88,000 my first year (which was a little less than my full-time salary). By the second year in business, my gross income grew 42% (mind you, I paid fellow independents who joined my projects) and it's increased every year since I started my company. The only year my income took a dip was in 2017 when I took a 12-week sabbatical—which is just one of the many perks of being my own boss.

I share this not to toot my own horn—although there is nothing wrong with that, but to paint a picture for you about what's possible.

What's in it for me?

Is this life for everyone? No. But, is it for more people than you'd think? I'd argue that the answer is yes—especially with the rise of the gig economy. If you've gotten this far, I'm guessing you are toying with the idea. This book can help you decide if it's right for you. And, if you are pretty sure you want to take the leap... read on—I'm here to help!

Here's what you'll walk away with after reading this book:

1. Details to decide if the independent life is the life for you
2. A road map for making the leap
3. Clear direction about the team of advisors you should put around you
4. A playbook for becoming an actual company

5. Suggestions on where and how to find business
6. How-tos for creating solid agreements with your clients

Along the way I'll share suggestions from my own experience, provide resources that you can tap into, and share advice and cautionary tales from other free agents who have so generously told me their stories over the years. Throughout the book you'll see these icons:

 Gretchen's Playbook: These are strategies I use every day to keep myself sane, my clients delighted, and my projects running like well-oiled machines.

 From the Trenches: One-hundred-sixteen independents from across the US, Canada, Turkey, Australia, New Zealand, India, the UK, and beyond shared what surprised them about being an independent, what they wish they would have known when they started, and the advice they would give to someone just beginning. I've sprinkled this gold dust throughout the book. And while I've changed their names, the wisdom comes directly from their hearts and minds.

 Handy Resources: These are books, articles, and TedTalks that I've found particularly helpful over the years.

 Word to the Wise: While I include lots of advice, when you see this icon, it connotes advice that if not taken to heart, could really put you in a sticky situation. Who wants that? Nobody.

No matter where you are in your journey or what you ultimately decide to do, I celebrate the fact that you are considering all your options. It is my great honor to play a small role in your decision-making process. Let's dig in, shall we?

Chapter
Two

The Good, the Bad, and the "Meh":

Deciding if the Gig Economy is Right for You

*A*s William Shakespeare said in *Hamlet*, "To be, or not to be, that is the question..." And that is, indeed, the question. There are many things to consider when making the decision to leap into the gig economy. Let's start with the first couple of factors.

First, are you clear in your own heart and mind about what you *really* want? And second, do you know what you're willing to give up?

These can be tough questions to answer and, if you're like me when I was contemplating making the leap, you might be wondering how to even go about answering them. My best advice? The more honest you get with yourself now, the better. And, if you are feeling overwhelmed by all of this... take a breath. You can only eat an elephant one fork full at a time, as they say (note, I would never eat an elephant... they are so cute!). Get your fork out and start chewing.

One thing that has surprised me about being an independent is that even with all the stresses, it is a wonderfully empowering way to live and work. ~ Penelope, 45, strategy consultant, New York, NY

There are three things I know for sure. First, realistically, you won't be able to answer all of these questions with absolute certainty. That's okay, educated guesses will do—and you're way ahead of people who don't even know to think about these things (Pat yourself on the back. Really. Pat yourself on the back. Now.).

Second, some of these questions you won't be able to answer until you're in the middle of it—I know, not an awesome feeling if you're a planner. But, no worries. Take it from me—a person who has plan for my plans—you'll figure it out!

And finally, the information, exercises, and advice in this book from me and many other brave and talented independents will help.

Plan as well as you can, but also be prepared to adapt and change as circumstances change. I think being able to adapt has been one of my greatest strengths as an independent contractor and it's also helped increase success. ~ Isabelle, 44, writer and editor, Chicago, IL

Tell me what you want, what you really, really want

If you're currently employed full-time and are deciding if you want to "shut down" that life and become a free agent, great! You'll need to consider what you're willing to give up.

If, on the other hand, you're in a situation where you've already been pushed off the ledge, or like me ten years ago... the ledge is in sight, then focus mostly on what you are gaining. But, no matter how you've arrived at this point, it's important for you to be clear about what you want.

I emphasize this because if you are not confident in your decision by the time you put yourself out there and declare to the world that you are in independent, no one else will be. And that will be a big problem when it comes to convincing people to hire you and give you money.

Over the years I've hired more than thirty fellow independents to join my teams. Our projects last anywhere from weeks to months. As I build my teams, it is not uncommon to run across reluctants who are just "stopping in" on the independent lifestyle. There is nothing wrong with this, but from my *own* experience, I want to hire someone who is committed to being an independent—at least as long as they have agreed to work on my project. Be sure to exude confidence and commitment about your chosen way of working when talking with prospective clients.

Be absolutely honest with people if you are currently interviewing for full-time work while you are consulting. This means you should not take projects that are more than a few weeks long so that you can easily roll off the project should your dream full-time position come along.

Or, you should commit to suspending your job search if you take a longer project. Leaving a client in the lurch is not a good idea. It could come back to bite you down the road should you find yourself back in the gig economy and, frankly, it's just not cool.

What you gain

I've been working this way for ten years, and I love it! Ask any independent why they like it and you'll hear many things.

- **Every day is bring-your-dog-to-work day.** My guy's name is Ocho and I love him—even when he barks while I am on conference calls.

- **I work based on my energy.** As a farm kid, it's in my DNA to rise early. My most productive hours are 6:00 to 10:00 a.m. When I worked in an office, I spent my most productive time getting ready for work, driving to work, chatting with people on my way to my cube, and often getting caught by people with "fires" to put out before I did *one thing* that was on my priority list. Now, I pad into my office and work in my P.J.s until I have a break in the morning and can shower (maybe) and get dressed.

- **Pick of the litter.** I have a tremendous amount of control over with whom I work. When it's a project I am running, I have total control because I'm building the team with my favorite colleagues who I trust and respect. When I am *joining* a team, I get to choose if I want to be part of that team—no one can assign me to anything or stick me on a team that has dead weight or underperformers. I also get to pick my clients. If I have a bad feeling about a prospect, I can gracefully decline to take the project. With all that said, there are times when I have to work with challenging personalities on the client side team, but exposure is usually limited and because I work with great clients, who often act as a buffer between my team and the internal team.

- **Autonomy.** In addition to being able to choose with whom I work, I decide each day how many hours I'm going to work, from where I am going to work—will I sit in my home office, work from the coffee shop, head to a library, sit on my deck? I also get to decide what new skills I want to learn and how I want to go about learning them—do I want to attend a webinar, go to a conference, take a class, read a book in the middle of the day? And, I have a ton of control over how much money I make.

I was surprised by how much I love being able to carve out time for my kids. From hanging out in the morning to attending daytime school events I missed in the past. ~ Jake, 50, leadership and business coach, Denver, CO

- **Every minute is more productive.** I won't even try to calculate the number of lost hours of work in the eight years I was a full-time employee between unwelcomed social interaction, company-wide events, and walls of meetings on my calendar every day. Some of it was necessary, but most of it was not. As an independent, you will likely not be asked to attend town hall meetings, team lunches, all staff meetings, and anniversary or birthday parties in the breakroom. You will have control over what meetings you attend, and which ones you take a pass on. And, while I like socializing as much as the next gal, I detest being interrupted when I am deep in thought—which happened at least *five* times a day while working in a cube farm.

- **In my first year of working independently, my dad stayed at my house for a week.** After watching me work for a few days he said, "I think you probably get more done before 10 a.m., than most people get done in a day." That remains one of the best compliments I've ever received and it was made all the better because it came from one of the people I respect most in this world.

- **Authenticity.** As an independent I don't have to worry about corporate culture and whether or not I am a fit. I spend absolutely zero energy trying to shape myself to fit in anywhere that does not feel right to me. In my full-time employment days, I remember getting coaching about how I should adjust so as not to ruffle feathers and to play the corporate politics game effectively—both very important things if you want to have a long shelf life inside a company. I lost more than one night of sleep worrying about whether I was doing something right. As an independent... I have had exactly zero conversations like this. With that said, I do make it a point at the start of a project to talk with clients about their corporate culture and how my team and I can support them in making sure feathers aren't being ruffled and corporate politics are being played well. But this lands differently on my spirit. It feels like I have a choice and I like I'm helping my clients shine—which is what gets me out of bed in the morning.

- **Instant credibility (most of the time).** Depending on the project and your role on the project, your voice comes with some built in validity because you are a consultant being paid to come in from the outside with an expert point of view—or at least a different perspective. I have found that as an outsider, I can play the I'm-new-here card and ask "stupid" questions, which often are the exact questions that need to be asked. And the beauty is that asking these questions is a service to clients who might not feel safe to ask such questions.

- **Always learning.** Being able to work in multiple organizations and across industries is a built-in antidote to burn out—at least for me. It is a true delight to be continually learning without having to look too hard. It appeals to the frustrated detective in me to unravel the puzzle of a new project and figure out what makes the client tick, identify the best solution set, and determine how the heck to get it done. I've learned things I never imagined I'd learn and have done things I never imagined—including crawling round in a tunnel wearing steel-toed shoes to observe an engineer using equipment that I then created training materials to teach others how to use. Fun times! Seriously.

When I first started out, I never expected how much flexibility I'd have in charting new paths. ~ Deven, 41, education consultant, Raleigh, NC

- **Projects come to an end.** Because (most of) the work we independents do is project-based and defined in a contract or statement of work, everything we work on has a clear beginning and a defined end. And boy, do I. Love. That! The "tidiness" of this work arrangement appeals to my need for organization. It also means that there is protection against the phenomenon of work that continues to pile onto the plate without Anything. Ever. Being taken off. You control how much is on your plate at any given time. And, for me, when I have piled too much onto my plate, it somehow feels less intolerable because I did it to myself. *And*, I can get myself out of the situation (eventually). Plus, if you find yourself in this situation, and have structured your contract well, at least you are pulling in the cash.

Being an independent means that you get to design your life. A few years ago, I decided to take a three-month sabbatical. I looked at how much money I needed to cover my expenses during my time off and how much I was going to have to work in order to put that money in the bank. I stopped work before Thanksgiving and didn't return until after Valentine's Day. I sailed in the Caribbean, read the newspaper every morning, did yoga every day, read three books, took two trips to visit family, and went on a road trip with my girlfriends. Ahh... sweet autonomy!

What you give up

So those are some of the things you'll likely get if you choose to make the leap. And, because we don't live in Utopia, there are things you give up. This is where it starts to get pretty real for people.

- **Steady pay check.** In academia, they say publish or perish. In the gig economy, it would be safe to say the mantra is produce or perish. If you aren't working, you aren't getting paid. Period. And, every client pays on a different timeline. I have some clients who pay within two weeks, others within thirty days, and I have one client who makes it their standard agreement that they only have to pay within sixty (60!) days of receiving an invoice. And then you have to deal with slowdowns in the invoicing process. I've, unfortunately heard, "Oh, I'm so sorry, I thought I submitted that," more than once.

1. Ideally, you'll have a few clients at any given time so if one client is slow in paying, cash is flowing in from elsewhere.

2. As you are putting the finishing touches on your contract, ask your client:

   a. What the invoicing process is. Do you submit to them or someone on their team who processes invoices? Do they need to be copied—anyone else? Does the invoice have to go to anyone besides them for approval?

   b. Are there any dollar thresholds that require extra layers of approval? If there are, you should structure your invoicing schedule so that invoices are written in small enough amounts to require the fewest number of approvals. I've had checks held up because the executive vice president was travelling for a month.

   c. Do they pay vendors through electronic funds transfer? If so, can you get set up? This can cut days out of the timeline for getting money in your hands, plus the cash hits your account even if you are out of town.

d. What sort of information and what level of detail do they need on the invoice in order to process? I've had invoices rejected by the powers that be because they needed a vendor number or a project code on the invoice. And well-meaning clients who don't understand the ins and outs of their organization's invoicing process can sometimes pass along invoices without specific details, only to find out two weeks after you submit that there is something missing. Which then kicks your invoice back to the bottom of the pile.

3. And, it might be obvious, but I'm going to say it anyway... have an emergency cash fund. I know this is not helpful if you are a reluctant and already thrust into the independent life. But, if you are still working, put a plan together to have at least three months (and six is better!) of cash on hand. This will make you feel—and run the risk of appearing—desperate.

Make a financial plan before you quit your full-time job! Have enough money so you don't have to take the first (horrid) project that comes your way. ~ Kelly, 70, consumer goods industry consultant, Chicago, IL

Have some work lined up before you leave your day job. Leave your day job on good terms—it could lead to work in the future. ~ Terry, 50, management consultant, Chicago, IL

If you have a partner, practice living on one salary for six months before you go independent. ~ Abigail, 47, learning strategy consultant, Evanston, IL

The need for financial security/planning. I underestimated the length of possible dry spells. They would have been navigable had I planned better. ~ Deven, 41, education consultant, Raleigh, NC

- **You supply your own benefits.** This can be a big blocker for people and is something to spend a fair amount of time thinking about and understanding the financial implications for your own financial situation. These are some of the biggest considerations.
  - **Health insurance.** This is one of the first things people ask me about when asking for advice on making the leap. The good news is that the Affordable Care Act (ACA) provides a fairly easy way to get health insurance—although the costs have increased and the plan options continue become more limited each year post-ACA. And at the time of this writing, there is a fair amount of uncertainty about what is going to happen with the ACA. You can expect to pay a significant amount more than you pay for your employer plan and you can likely count on having a fairy high deductible to keep your premiums lower. In 2018, I am paying (just for me) $378.00 a month, and have a limited number of providers to choose from (but, am in a good network in case something really bad happens), and I have a $6,000 deductible (ouch). Honestly, health insurance is the only part of being an independent that I despise. I've just come to expect that it's a necessary evil to give me access to all that good things I mentioned above. And, I am crossing my fingers that a knight and shining armor swoops in (with a kick-ass insurance policy) and pops the question! Some people marry for green cards, in the future, I

predict people will marry for health insurance. Kidding, not kidding.

- **Dental and Eye insurance.** These policies are sold separately. I know many independents who go without and pay out of pocket. I choose to have dental—which I am pay about $23 a month. In the end, if all I do are two cleanings a year, it ends up being a wash. But, in a chocolate-heavy year I might have a cavity—which usually means my dental insurance saves me some money. In terms of eye insurance, I buy a policy in a year when I know I am going to want to get my eyes checked and then skip it the following year. My policy usually runs me about $150 for the year. As I age, I might have to do this annually, but for now this works.

- **Disability insurance.** When you strike out on your own, there is no short or long-term disability insurance. If you want it, you have to buy your own policy. Up to this point I have chosen not to carry either of these, although my financial planner and I agreed that at 45 I should pull the trigger. Again, if you are not working because of an accident or health issue, you are not getting paid. You'll have to decide for yourself what sort of risks you are willing to take. If you participate in edgy activities like riding your bike though the streets of a big city, then you might want to purchase short-term insurance. I won't lie, I've been a very careful skier and sailor since I went independent. Policies are based on age, habits, and where you live. You can go to any disability insurance provider and run numbers using their online calculator.

- **Unemployment insurance.** Nope. None of that. If work dries up, the unemployment office has zero interest in your situation. Another reason it is good to have three to six months of cash on hand for emergencies.

- **Social Security and Medicare.** You've likely noticed that money

goes out of your check and toward Social Security and Medicare.
What you may not know is that one benefit of full-time employment
is that your employer pays half of these taxes. Once you go
independent, Uncle Sam will ask you to pay the whole she-bang.
How much you owe will depend on your taxable income. The good
news is that some of this is deductible and any good accountant can
help you navigate this.

You can do it. Taxes are inevitable. Just go for it. And have a solid six
months of living expenses tucked away. ~Ginny, 47, eLearning developer,
Boulder, CO

Get an accountant now. ~Nina, marketing consultant, Largo, FL

○ **Leave—personal, vacation, holidays.** If you want to take days off,
you have to plan for it (more on that later). I have consistently taken
four weeks of vacation a year. I usually build my vacations around
national holidays—when I know clients won't be working—and
slower times in my sales cycle. In my industry, things get slow by
mid-December and then start perking up with new budgets toward
the end of January. I also have quite a few clients whose fiscal years
end in August which means July and August are busy with people
trying to spend money and September and October are busy because
they have new money to spend. So, I try to be fully billable during
those months.

○ **Leave—sick, family, bereavement.** There is no avoiding it. Life
happens. And while you can't avoid it, you can plan for it. And the
longer you are in the gig economy, the more likely *something* will

happen. During my ten years as an independent, I went through a divorce, my mother had her bladder removed, my father had a heart attack, I took a bad fall down some icy steps that took months of recovery, and at least once a year, I get hit with the flu or a bad cold. Do yourself a favor and plan for the inevitable so that when it happens, you can be fully present for yourself and for whomever you might be provided care.

1. **Stay healthy.** Any medical professional will tell you to do the following because it's good for your health. I am telling you for business reasons, because if you don't work, you don't eat. Intentionally do things to keep yourself healthy. I take vitamins, have a fairly strict sleep schedule, (I try to) eat well, watch my caffeine intake in the afternoons, and I do yoga—I have a yoga mat laid out in my office at all times.

2. **Try to work regular hours.** Having the autonomy to choose when you work can be a double-edged sword. Sure, you can work whenever you want, but the hours can fly off the clock and before you know it, you've been sitting at your desk for twelve hours. Hopefully, I don't need to explain why that is not healthy. I usually start work anytime between 6:00 and 7:30 a.m. and then end my day by 3:00-3:30 in the afternoon. Because I am an early riser, this works for me. It allows me to work a solid nine-hour day (if I need to), but ending at 3:30 still helps me feel like I have a lot of time to do things like workout, cook dinner, and hang out with friends.

3. **Keep six months of cash in the bank.** Not to beat this drum too much, but let me beat this drum too much... It is a blessing to have the flexibility to help family in times of crisis—another perk of being

an independent—but, if you are feeling stressed about money, it will likely be hard for you to provide the help and support you want.

4. **Find ways to save for retirement.** Remember, there's no company-sponsored 401k. Saving for retirement is completely on you. The biggest drawback is that if you are currently at a company where there is a match that goes away. The good news is that you can set up a Solo or Individual 401K—and you get a lot of the same tax benefits that you get with your company sponsored 401K. The tricky part is that you have to write the check each month—no automatic deduction from your paycheck before you even see it.

5. **Find ways to cope with isolation.** This can be a big one for some people. I know independents who return to an office job fairly quickly because they really missed the built-in social interaction in an office. And others, like me, don't miss it one bit. Personally, I plan a lunch or two a week. The beauty is that these are lunch dates with people I *really* want to see at restaurants I love rather than some of the more obligatory lunches I had to participate in in my full-time working days. I also head to the gym or yoga a few times a week in the late afternoons. This gets me out of the house and gets my body moving. Win, win!

6. **Remember to budget for your professional development.** The great news is that your first few years as an independent will present you with so many opportunities to learn stuff, you won't feel bummed about not growing. But, if you are used to attending the big annual conferences for your industry, you're going to have to budget for it and write the check. I tend to budget for the big conferences every two to three years, and then try to take advantage of local events. I also check the chapter events of my industry's associations in the places I am vacationing or visiting family. Doing this can be a great way to build your network, learn a thing or two, and you can write off a

portion of your travel.

I thought I might miss an office environment. I don't. AT ALL. ~ Abigail, 47, learning strategist, Evanston, IL

I didn't think I would miss the "water cooler talk." But I did. ~ Kelly, 70, consumer goods industry consultant, Chicago, IL

I was surprised at how disciplined I am working alone. ~ Stuart, 60, medical studies research assistant, Boston, MA

I didn't expect how much I enjoy working with teams sometimes and then being able to work on my own at home other times. ~ Lucinda, 53, media consultant, Los Angeles, CA

I was surprised to discover that I do not miss working in an office. ~ Tanya, 48, graphic designer, Indianapolis, IN

Challenges of the gig economy

There are pros and cons when it comes to joining the gig economy. But, there is also this stuff in the middle that most people you ask about this lifestyle might not think to mention. None of these factors are big enough, in my opinion, to tip the balance of your decision either way. But, in the spirit of sharing the good, the bad, and the meh... here's the "meh."

- **Riding the cash flow roller coaster.** There are ups. There are downs. This reality never goes away. But how you ride through it depends on how well you plan. In addition to having a cash reserve of three to six months of expenses, it's a good idea to save along the way. As Kate, 57 and a graphic designer from Dallas, TX said, "You have to be okay with not getting a regular paycheck. You will have good years (save, save) and lean years. If you save, you will be okay. No one wants to hire a desperate consultant."

1. **Figure out your monthly expenses.**

2. **Set up a business bank account into which you deposit all income from clients.**

3. **Set up a regular pay day where you transfer the same amount each time from your business checking account to your personal checking account. Live within that amount until your next pay day.** I recommend simulating what you are used to—typically, every other week or the last business day of a month. That way you are not "dipping into" your business account often. If you set things up this way and then find yourself dipping into your business account or changing the amount you pay yourself between pay days, consider that a red flag. Something is not working with your money management. Armed with that kind of insight, you can adjust (either work more or spend less) sooner rather than later.

- **The ebb and flow of workload.** While cash flow can feel like a roller coaster, so can managing your workload. Most independents have to go through twelve to eighteen months before they really understand how much work they can take on at any given time and how much is too much. And, if you are feeling stressed about money, you'll more than likely experience the crunch of committing to too much work.

And, you'll probably find yourself in that spot more than a few times.

1. **Map out a high-level timeline with estimated time and effort each week of the duration of the project before you sign the contract.** Look at how that work stacks up against the other work on your plate.

2. **Be realistic about what you are willing to do in order to make it work.** Do not be overly optimistic about what is possible. The worst thing you can do is commit to something and then deliver late or deliver an inferior product. The fastest way to a cash flow crunch is to have a client not hire you again.

3. **Plan for time off.** Don't forget about your upcoming vacations and family commitments.

4. **Understand not all time is billable.** Don't forget to factor in time you have to spend working on your business (invoicing, selling, networking), not just in your business.

5. **Know the power of assumptions.** Once you are confident that you can promise a specific timeline, build your assumptions into the agreement. For example, if you are working on an hourly contract and you are assuming you'll work anywhere from 10-20 hours a week on a project, you should say that. Then, if the project is growing or changing (as they always do), and therefore putting you in a crunch, you can easily talk with your client about the initial assumption. Then, together you can reset expectations.

6. **Understand your ideal workload.** After 10 years, I have learned my sweet spot is to have three-four projects going at any given time and that I spend 4-6 hours a week on non-billable work. This is going to be different for everyone, but it's a good idea to track your time for the

first year to really get a handle on how much time different tasks take.

7. **Know when to raise your rates.** Finally, if your services are that much in demand, it might be a sign that you should raise your rates.

- **Navigating the burnout culture.** If not managed, burnout can be a constant threat. While I have never felt burnt out by the actual work I do, I have teetered on the edge of crashing and burning because I did not manage the ebb and flow of workload (see above). As an independent, you must build in boundaries or you can easily work every waking minute. I hope I don't have to tell you that is not sustainable. But, just in case... THAT IS NOT SUSTAINABLE. Clients do not have visibility into how much you work, how much time different tasks take, and what it is going to take for you to fulfill on the objectives of the project. They will let you work yourself into the ground—often times not even realizing they are doing so. It is incumbent upon you to communicate with your clients about what is possible and, when necessary, adjust expectations so that you don't break.

- **Fear.** I'm talking about wake-you-from-a-deep-sleep fear. It can come from anywhere and can happen as a result of any combination of things. It could be rooted in money—either not having it now, or being worried it's going to dry up and you won't have it later. It could come from a client who is not happy about something. And, it could come as a result of a resource you've hired that is not producing how you planned. Sound familiar? It should. It's a lot of the same stuff that probably keeps you or kept you up during your full-time employment days. The big difference as independent is that there is nowhere to hide and there is no one coming to help you get out of the situation.

1. **The easiest thing is to what you can to keep yourself out of stressful situations.** Don't take on more work than you can deliver on. Don't undercharge for your services. Create clear client agreements with explicit assumptions that you are making.

2. **Find a group of supportive colleagues who spend their days in the gig economy.** Reach out to one and share your concerns. Often times simply talking with someone can help relieve the pressure. They can remind you, if you can't remind yourself, that it always works out.

3. **Rely on the past.** Once you get a few cycles under your belt, I find it's useful to remind myself that I have had this exact same fear and I got through it. Be as specific with yourself as possible. It might sound like this:

   a. "Okay self, last January you were worried that no new projects were showing up and that come March, you were going to have no work. You reached out to a couple past clients to let them know you had open capacity and attended two networking events. You ended up starting one new project in February and a second new project in March."

   b. "Okay, self, you have six months of cash in the bank for this exact reason. If the worst thing happens and no projects show—which that has never happened—and no new projects show up when this current project ends, you will be fine. You've never gone more than a few days with no work. Take a breath."

- **Crisis of confidence.** A crisis of confidence is when you are faced with a task/project/problem that you've never encountered and have no idea how to even begin to tackle it. And, beyond that, you have a moment that can last minutes or hours (hopefully, not days) where you actually believe you will not be able to figure it out. I'm sure I'd felt this prior to my days as an independent, but never as acutely. I think it's because working independently means that you usually do not have instant access to a group of colleagues with whom to bounce things off. I have three colleagues who do the exact same work I do who are my go-to people when I run into these moments. They can be counted on to remind me that I am capable and can ask me a few questions to get me unstuck. And, the beauty is that *I* am *their* phone-a-friend when *they* have their crisis of confidence. I can also tell you that these moments have gotten farther apart over the years.

- **Being viewed as not big enough.** Depending on the work you do, it is possible that you will run into potential clients who hesitate to hire an independent or an independent who is building a team of fellow independents. The good news is that this hesitation is becoming less of an issue as more talented people join the ranks of the gig economy. But, for the foreseeable future, some of us will continue to run into this. I've combated this by getting a couple lucky breaks early to run big projects with my merry band of independents. A proven track record is often enough to help prospects get over this concern.

- **Flexing to multiple processes.** Again, depending on the work you do, you might find yourself working with multiple clients who ask you to work within their business process. For example, right now I have three clients who have each given me a laptop. They want me to send email using my gretchen.hartke@ClientCompany.com email address. They also want me to upload my working files into their file sharing software—which all work differently and require different log in information. This can get a little unwieldy if you are not organized. When I am in these situations, I set clear expectations that I will not be monitoring those inboxes all day and that if the client really needs to get to me quickly, they should text me and ask me to check my email. I also ask them NOT to copy all my email addresses on an email—which doubles the amount of email I have to dig through.

- **Difficult conversations are unavoidable.** This is true no matter what your working life looks like, but I found the quantity of tough conversations increased when I became an independent. It is inevitable that a client is going to want or think one thing and you are going to want and think another thing. Or, you'll hire a fellow independent to work on your project and they just aren't getting the work done as you expected. The ability to have authentic, tough conversations is a good skill to develop. I recommend reading of *Crucial Conversations: Tools for Talking when Stakes are High* by Patterson, Grenny, McMillian, and Switzler. I also suggest that you find a trusted colleague to role-play or talk through how you are planning to address the situation. I've found that a little coaching and a pep talk can go a long way.

- **Confronting other people's assumptions about your time.** Maya, 37, a strategic communications consultant from Atlanta shared, "I've been surprised by the perception of others that I don't work. It's laughable but still offensive." It's true that as an independent, you will likely run into people that assume they can benefit from your flexibility. I've had people in my building assume I could be the go-to person to let maintenance people in, organizations I volunteer with who assume I can meet during business hours, and have had to adjust my family's assumptions about how available I am during my working hours. Developing the ability to set boundaries and reshape assumptions will help you protect your precious billable time.

- **Administrative minutiae.** You likely want to jump into the gig economy to do specific work—which you'll get to do a lot of. But, there is also a lot of "other stuff" you'll have to spend time doing—invoicing and chasing invoices that have not been paid, talking with your accountant, expense tracking in your accounting software, dealing with annoying technical issues, writing proposals, updating your website, getting business cards printed, dealing with the bank, and on and on.

Understand that there is a good deal of administrative work and recordkeeping in addition to what you do. ~ Mateo, 73, tax preparer, Santa Monica, CA

I wish I would have known how time consuming the 'back end' stuff would be-- billing, taxes, marketing, shipping. All the not fun stuff. ~ Lucinda, 53, media freelancer, Los Angeles, CA

Great! You're still here. Hopefully that means that you are excited about the good stuff that comes with being an independent and feel, at least on some level, that you can handle the not so good stuff.

The McKinsey Global Institute study reports that free agents who choose the gig economy report being more satisfied in 12 of the 14 dimensions measured than those working in traditional full-time jobs. These areas of satisfaction include:

- Topics/activities working on
- Overall work life
- Number of hours worked
- Independence of work life
- Atmosphere at workplace
- Liking one's boss (naturally!)
- Level of empowerment

- Creativity one can express at work
- Ability to choose working hours
- Opportunities to learn, grow, and develop
- Flexibility regarding where work happens
- Recognition received

Not surprisingly, the two areas where satisfaction dipped slightly, were income security and income level. And while the gig economy is not for everyone and is not without its downside, MBO Partners, a service provider supporting self-employed professionals, reports in their 2017 *The State of Independence in America* study that 84 percent of full-time independents surveyed say they are happier working on their own than in a traditional job and 70 percent of that same group said working on their own is better for their health.

Chapter Three

Do You Have What It Takes?:

Skills Every Independent Needs Transition

Determining if you can live with the good, the bad, and the "meh" of the gig economy is one part of deciding if it's right for you. The other part is taking an honest look inwardly at yourself and the inner workings of your personal and professional life.

- Do you have the characteristics that successful independents exhibit? And, if you don't, can you see yourself realistically growing in some new areas?

- Do you know what you are going to offer to the world and do   you know if people will pay you for this service or product?

- Have you run the numbers? Do you know how much you need to make and have you looked at what you realistically think you can make?

Do you have the right stuff?

The good news is that there isn't just one personality composite that can be a successful independent. I know highly successful independents who are extroverts *and* introverts, off-the-wall creatives *and* buttoned-up analytical thinkers, and everything in between. And, no matter your personality type, there is a consistent set of traits that successful independents seem to have.

Place a check mark next to any of following statements that describe you.

____I can do anything if given enough time and information.

____I am motivated when someone likes the work I have done.

____I've never met a problem I didn't want to tackle.

____I can live without getting a job promotion.

____I love it when I look up from a project I am working on and see that two hours have flown off the clock.

____I frequently write to-do lists.

____I usually check off the high priority items on my to-do list each week.

____I can shift my approach—be it tone, style, humor, body language—given the situation or environment I'm in.

____I love having a plan for the day, and I am okay if priorities shift.

____I can ask for what I need.

____I am more likely to ask a question than give an opinion.

____If asked, I could tell someone what I am good at.

____I don't have to have everything figured out before I start trying to solve a problem.

____When I send emails asking for things, I usually get what I need from others.

____When I make a mistake, I'll be the first one to point it out.

____When I am uncomfortable with something, I can speak up.

There is no magic number of how many of these you should check, but if you placed a checkmark next to most of these statements, there is a good chance that you have a personality that will work well in the gig economy. Here is a round-up of the things that I believe make me, and the independents I respect and trust, successful.

Grit. Firmness of mind or spirit: unyielding courage in the face of hardship or danger. (Merriam-Webster)

- **Why it matters:** This is the "stuff" inside you that helps you keep going as you pursue your goals. It goes beyond what you know and what you've already done. This is what helps you push through the uncomfortable parts of being an independent as you move forward.

- **When it comes in handy:**
  - Anytime you are faced with something new that you've never done and that scares you a little (or a lot!)
  - When a client comes to you with a problem that is fuzzy and ambiguous, and you just aren't sure where to start
  - When someone is questioning your ability, knowledge, position, direction, etc.
  - In those dark moments when you are not sure you can do what you've set out to do

Really think about whether you can cope with the fluctuating income and workload and the fact that the only person who can motivate you is yourself. ~ Sid, 30, freelance writer and communications specialist, Auckland, New Zealand

- Watch Angela Duckworth's TedTalk, *Grit: The Power of Passion and Perseverance*.
- Read her book with the same title.

Action oriented. Using practical methods which involve *doing* things to deal with problems, not just *talking* about ideas, plans, or theories. (Merriam-Webster)

- **Why it matters:** Occasionally, depending on your area of expertise, clients might pay you to simply be a thought partner, but most likely, the majority of your billable time is going to be tied to actually *doing* things. So, your ability to jump in quickly and start getting things done is critical to being able to put food on the table.

- **When it comes in handy:**
  - At the start of a project when you want to have a quick win or prove your value early on
  - When current projects are coming to an end and you need to find your next gig
  - In those moments when you are feeling paralyzed by stress or fear—a lot of times just "getting into action" is the antidote
  - Every day as you prioritize your work

- Watch Tim Urban's TedTalk, *Inside the Mind of a Master Procrastinator*
- Read Kevin Kruse's book, *15 Secrets Successful People Know About Time Management*

Self-motivated. Initiative to undertake or continue a task or activity without another's prodding or supervision. (Dictionary.com)

- **Why it matters:** Obviously, as an independent, there is no boss or manager holding you accountable. It's all on you to drive yourself each day. Sure, your clients are expecting you to hit your deadlines, but they aren't invested in how or when it happens—just that it happens as expected.
- **When it comes in handy:**
  - When facing the tasks on your to-do list—especially the tasks that are not billable or directly tied to a project. No one but you *really* cares about whether these tasks are completed, but *you know* they will make a difference for your business. Things like writing a blog

post for your website or creating a branded invoice rather than using the generic invoice generated in Quickbooks

- ○ In lieu of getting a job promotion. Once you become an independent, your title does not change—unless you change it, and if you do, no one cares or notices. If you've been motivated by promotions in the past, you will not have that construct as an independent. You'll have to find different makers of progress like landing a specific client or a project that generates X amount of revenue.
- ○ When you'd like someone to say, "great job!" But, because you work alone there is no one who even sees it.

1. I literally have an Outlook folder called, "Kudos." I put any emails from clients where they've expressed satisfaction about something, and even an "atta girl" or two from my dad. I'll dive into that folder and re-read when I am needing a little morale boost.

2. Toward the end of a project, ask clients to write a LinkedIn review.

3. Praise someone else. Sometimes if I need an ego boost and it's not coming my way, I simply praise someone else for the awesome work they are doing. Often, acknowledging someone else's job-well-done feels better than having someone tell me that I am doing a great job.

Organized. Able to plan things carefully. (Cambridge)

- **Why it matters:** All the action orientation and self-motivation in the world won't amount to much if you can't plan your work and work your plan. And this goes for *all* of your work. This includes project deliverables, networking, selling, invoicing, collecting your money, cleaning your work space, getting your taxes paid (on time!), and the hundreds of other things you have to do to make your business run each day, week, month, and year.

- **When it comes in handy:**
  - Every minute of every day. They say the whole is a sum of its parts, and that's true with all the small decisions you have to make and the many things you have to do in any given day. The more organized you are, the more you will accomplish.
  - When creating a realistic to-do list and getting to the end of it each week
  - Making sure cash is flowing as steadily as possible
  - Ensuring you are following up on the things that are not the highest priority. For example, following up on sales leads even when you are in the thick of getting work done on a current project
  - Carving out time to rest, relax, and recharge

You have to be able to work without much direction, so if you're disorganized or can't solve problems on your own, it may not be the right career path. ~ Seiko, 61, medical editor working in the pharmaceutical industry, Trenton, NJ

Make sure you figure out how to factor in true down time. It's so hard to turn it off when the buck stops with you. ~ Ted, 44, media freelancer, Bloomington, IN

Effective communicator. One that communicates in such a way that it produces a decided, decisive, or desired effect. (Merriam-Webster)

- **Why it matters:** No matter what you do, I'll bet it involves a lot of words to get from the beginning to the end of your work each day. In *Science*, University of Arizona professor of Psychology, Matthias

Mehl, published the results of a study indicating that men and women speak an average 16,000 words a day. And, the Radicati Group, a telecommunications market research firm, published a 2017 study that estimates 296 billion emails are sent every day, which works out to about 72 emails per person. That's a lot of words. And, if your livelihood depends on how well you use your 16,000 spoken words and your 72 emails a day, you better be able to do it well.

- **When it comes in handy:**
  - When trying to cut through the daily clutter being hurled at your clients from multiple sources. You don't want to be the person who makes your client cringe when they see your name pop up in their inbox.
  - Getting quick responses and decisions from your clients
  - Convincing prospects that you understand their issues and that you can deliver a solution that solves their problem

- If you lack confidence when it comes to public speaking, find a coach like Mikki Williams (www.mikkiwilliams.com) or Diane DiResta (www.diresta.com)
- Watch Celeste Headlee's TedTalk, *10 Ways to Have a Better Conversation*
- Search for "Google's tips for writing emails" to see nine techniques for communicating via email used by executives at Google

Assertive. Behaving confidently and being able to say in a direct way what you want or believe. (Cambridge)

- Why it matters: Being an independent means that in a lot of ways, the world is your oyster. You can take your work and your business in a lot of different directions. There is extraordinary freedom in this. And there is a real danger. You have to be careful to not unwittingly go down a path that is not in alignment with what you want: be it, how you want to work, the kind of work you want to do, deciding with whom to work, or how much you want to get paid. You are your only advocate because, well, it's just you. If you don't speak up, no one else will. And, that is a surefire way to get yourself into many undesirable situations.

- **When it comes in handy:**
  - Being able to sell yourself and your value clearly and confidently
  - Asking for what you need—be it things like the rate you want to be paid, your willingness to work onsite (or not), or the tools you're willing to use to complete your work
  - Speaking up when a project or an element of a project is not going as planned or as understood from your perspective

- Watch Luvvie Ajayi's TedTalk, *Get Comfortable with Being Uncomfortable*
- Read Travis Bradberry's book, *Emotional Intelligence 2.0*

Flexible. Characterized by a ready capability to adapt to new, different, or changing requirements. (Merriam-Webster)

- **Why it matters:** As important as it is to be assertive and aware of what you are or are not willing to do, you must also be equal parts flexible. As an independent, you will wear many hats both inside and outside your business. Your willingness to be flexible will keep you open to possibilities that you might not even be imagining at this point. When I first started out, I did not imagine that I would be running projects with $500K plus budgets and teams of six to ten people. But it turned out that I was really good at running highly complex projects. So, here I am, doing just that.

- **When it comes in handy:**
  - In those moments when your client needs a partner they can count on to get something done that no one else can do for them
  - As you move from client to client. Each person or organization you work for will have its own culture. You'll be more successful if you can bend or flex your personal style to fit in (at least a little) with them.
  - When an opportunity to build a new skill pops up

To be successful, be prepared to work very hard in order to gain as much experience in order to buy credibility and showcase versatility. ~ Patrick, 53, hospitality industry PR consultant, St. Charles, IL

Don't expect to have "no boss." Instead of one, you will end up having many! ~ Trelinda, 57, freelance tech industry writer and editor, Victoria, BC, Canada

Curious. Marked by desire to investigate and learn. (Merriam-Webster)

- **Why it matters:** I often feel like I am a bit of a detective or a doctor when I first start talking with a client about a prospective project. In order to understand the problem a client is trying to solve and to accurately scope the work, you have to ask a lot of questions. And then once you ask a question, *stop talking* and listen!

- **When it comes in handy:**
  - Every time you meet someone new. Most people like to share details about themselves and what they care about. I believe it's a gift to ask people great questions. Plus, you might find out that they have a need for which you are the perfect solution!
  - During initial sales conversations. The more you explore, the easier it will be to connect the dots for why *you are* a perfect fit.
  - While writing proposals or statements of work. The more information you collect up front, the more accurate your proposal will be and the more likely you'll be to close the deal.
  - During client meetings. Often times because you are coming with an outside perspective, you'll see things or ask questions that the internal team is a bit (or a lot) blind to. Being curious is an edge.
  - When seeking clarity. Depending on the work you do, it's possible that your work will start as a fuzzy bunch of information. Your curiosity and ability to ask questions is just the solution for bringing the fuzziness into focus.

- Watch Mike Vaughn's TedTalk, *How to Ask Better Questions*
- Read Peter Block's, *Flawless Consulting: A Guide to Getting Your Expertise Used*

Focused. Giving a lot of attention to one particular thing. (Merriam-Webster)

- **Why it matters:** I mentioned that autonomy is one of the good things about being an independent. And *it is*! However, there is a dark side. There are about a million and one things each day that can pull you away from the task at hand. Being organized and self-motivated will help make this easier. But, most independents will tell you that they do specific things each day to make sure they stay focused. If you don't, your precious billable hours might drift away.

- **When it comes in handy:**
  - When you need to think deeply. If you are a knowledge worker, you likely need chunks of time to think and do your work. Organization will help you carve out the time, but it's your ability to focus that will give you the goods and allow you to surface the quality of work for which your clients hired you. This is critical because it's your brain and your expertise that give you an edge and allow you to stay valuable and viable. But, unless you allow yourself to focus, you won't leverage this edge.

  - When you have your plan and it's time to execute. Imagine this: You've blocked out two hours this morning to write a proposal for a new client. You know it's going to take some time to comb through your portfolio of work and pull out samples that will really resonate. *And* it's going to take you some deep thinking to connect the dots succinctly and effectively for how your past work sets you up to be the perfect fit. And then the phone rings... it's your friend who is going through a personal crisis. Or, right before you are supposed to work, you take a look at your inbox and there are 15 new messages—how did that happen!? Or, your spouse calls and reminds you that you need to call the exterminator. Or, there are dishes in the sink from breakfast. Or... The reality is that you have to be disciplined enough to stick with your plan and protect your precious time.

Structure your days. Set up tasks for your week on a Sunday night. Actually allocate them to days and if you're super organised, to time slots. ~ Francis, 42, voice over talent, Bristol, United Kingdom

One thing that surprised me is the incredible amount of time, discipline, and focus that is required to be successful. ~ Carol, 47, grant writing consultant, Evansville, IN

Authentic. Representing one's true nature or beliefs; true to oneself. (Merriam-Webster)

- **Why it matters:** As an independent, you are your brand. The more you that you are in any given moment, the more likely you will be able to listen and be present for your clients. And, the more easily people will be able to connect to you beyond the surface. I believe that ultimately, we are humans working with and for other humans. Therefore, the more human and real you are, the more delightful the experience of working with you will be. Unless you are a sucky human. In that case, life as an independent will likely be short-lived. But, I know you aren't a sucky human because you are here, deeply considering if the independent consultant life is the life for you.
- **When it comes in handy:**
  - When you are meeting new people. If you are truly present in any moment with other people, they will feel heard. And, people like to be around other people who really hear them
  - In any interaction with clients and team members. Work should be fun and engaging. I find that humans are fun (most of the time) and engaging (all of the time), when they are showing up as real
  - When things go wrong. Mistakes are going to happen. Hopefully they won't be big ones, but no matter what... you must be honest and you

have to be sincere and authentic when you shine the light on the mistake. It may not make it easier, but if you are not authentic, it will *for sure* make the conversation even more uncomfortable

Thanks to Anna Belyaev, my former boss and mentor-for-life, I include the following risk in every project kickoff's list of risks and opportunities, "We are humans." I go on to explain that "at some point in this project any one of us, and probably each of us, will show up as being human—someone might get sick, we will take vacations, family emergencies might arise, priorities might shift at the last minute requiring a change in schedule, and it's very possible that a mistake may be made or a ball might get dropped."

I go on to explain that, "I've been doing this work long enough to know that this will happen and when it does, we'll raise our hands and say, 'I'm having a human moment.'"

By doing this, it sets the tone from the start that while we'll aim to be perfect, it's possible that some days perfect won't quite happen. It helps a type A personality like me have a bit of a safety net from myself and gives everyone on the team a little room to breathe when life happens.

If you haven't listened to Brené Brown's TedTalks or read any of her books, you should. Start with her TedTalk, *The Power of Vulnerability*.

Do you do something that has value to others?

Unless you are independently wealthy, at the end of the day, you must have a service or product for which people will pay. This seems obvious, but there are some classic mistakes new independents make:

- Attempting to turn a personal passion or hobby into a business without really understanding the market place.

- Making a career shift from one area of expertise into a brand new one and then setting off on your own *before* you have established yourself as someone who does the thing you are trying to do.

- Not having a clear understanding of your offering, so therefore, not being able to articulate for others what it is you do, and why they should give you money to do it.

Turning a hobby into a job

Let me be clear... I am not suggesting that you should not do this. I am *all for* loving what you do. However, if you can't make enough money doing what you love, then your life as an independent will likely be very short lived. It is also possible that if you try to turn something you love into a job, then that thing that once gave you such joy becomes, well... work.

Here is an example from my first failed attempt at a side hustle. Sixteen years ago, I used to LOVE scrapbooking. I could spend hours at the dining room table pouring over page layouts to capture and represent my memories in the most clever and creative ways. I loved it so much that I started a business called, Heartfelt Designs. I put up a website, developed processes around how to capture people's stories, and then turn them into scrapbooks for their families to enjoy.

There were a few fatal flaws to this plan. First, the amount of time it took me to create one scrapbook page and what people were *willing to pay* for one scrapbook page, were way out of whack. Second, while flow set in quickly while I was working on my own memories, it was not quite as fun and absorbing when it was someone else's memories. Third, as it turned out, people who value having scrapbooks already made their own—so there really was not much of a market.

At the end of the day, that sweet little plan of mine fizzled out and I stuck with my day job. Although, I still love looking at *my* scrapbooks!

If you fall into this category, here are some key questions you should answer before you take the plunge:

- Do people want your service?
- How many people are realistically willing to pay for your service in any given week, month, or year?
- How much are they willing to pay for it? Is that enough to keep food on your table and a roof over your head?
- How easy will it be to find customers or clients?
- How many other people already do what you are trying to do?
- What do you have to offer that is new or different from the people who are already in the space?
- Is it really something you would love doing for other people?

I know photographers, artists, greeting card makers, and writers who have built thriving businesses doing what they love. And there are a multitude of books out there that can help you think through the ins and outs of turning a hobby into a business. Read them, do your research, and be realistic.

Shifting careers

Again, I am not saying don't do this. There are plenty of people who take this very approach and find great success. What I will tell you is that taking this approach can feel like an uphill battle. If you are in this situation you can easily find yourself in a position of defending and justifying what the heck you are doing and why the heck someone should take a chance on you, when you are new to the game.

Despite having started a few businesses before, the amount of time spent networking and selling was surprising. This was a career change and my old network wasn't as fruitful as I had hoped. ~ Jake, 50, leadership and business coach, Denver, CO

About five years ago, I seriously toyed with taking my career in a completely different direction. I had a great idea to create facilitated outdoor adventure experiences for families in order to create a deeply connected experience for each family who attended a trip. I was so serious that I spent a year and quite a bit of money becoming a Certified Parent Coach™ through the Parent Coaching Institute. I also found a potential business partner, and invested money and time in market research.

I still believe it's a great idea and would make a difference in the lives of parents and children (please steal it and turn it into something wonderful!), but here is where I landed...

- To start that business, it would have taken an incredible amount of time and money to start up. And I already had a thriving business. Frankly, I did not want to start all over or take the financial hit during my high-earning 40s.

When I stood back and really looked at it, I realized that not only would it have impacted my standard of living at the time, but it would have also decreased the amount of money I was saving (and building upon through retirement investments), putting my retirement years at risk. Neither sacrifice felt right for me and my personal financial goals.

- There was an exorbitant amount of liability and a high level of complexity involved with starting that business. Again, I already had a thriving business with a proven business model. At the end of the day, the risks were just not worth it to me.

- I'm not a parent. As I started down the path of researching the idea, I was always asked to explain why I, as a non-parent, would be able and interested in having a business that focused on kids and family. This was not a show-stopper for me as I was confident I could craft a founder's story that made sense to people—former camp counselor, teacher, lover of children, and well, I was actually a child and grew up in a family—but, it was still annoying that I had to continually justify why *I was capable of doing such a thing.*

If you are a person contemplating a career shift, consider the following:

- Why? Seriously, why make the shift? What is happening in your current career that has you contemplating such a move?

- If you are contemplating making a complete switch, is it because you are bored with your current career? If so, before you jettison the whole shebang, consider if there is a way to re-energize what you are doing or parlay that expertise into an independent life.

- Is there a way to get some experience and build credibility before you put your entire livelihood on the line?

- And all those questions raised in the section above regarding whether people will pay you for the service, how much they will pay, and who else is already doing what you want to do?

Articulating what you do

Once you've looked long and hard at what you want to do, why you want to do it, and how likely it is that people will pay you for it, you've got to be able to explain it to others. If you can't clearly articulate what it is that you do and how it matters to others, your telephone will be very quiet and your inbox will be very empty.

As you consider your explanation, you may have a few ways to describe it based on whom you are talking with. For example, here is how I talk about my business:

- If I am talking with someone outside my industry, I might say, "My company creates training programs for other companies. You know... corporate training."

- If I am talking with someone within my industry who works in a smaller business, I might say, "I'm an instructional designer with a small custom learning company that creates learning experiences for companies like yours."

- If I am talking with someone within a Fortune 500 company who is in my industry, I might say, "We work with client organizations like yours to create and execute strategic learning initiatives."

If you are having a hard time articulating what you do, it might be because you are not entirely clear on your offering. Keep refining until it is clear to you and to others. And, make sure that it is *clear that you have an expertise* and that *you love the work.* If you are unable to sell those two things, it will be hard for prospective clients to take you seriously.

Build your professional capital around a niche or a few services. That allows you to become an expert and not a jack of all trades. ~Deven, 41, education consultant, Raleigh, NC

Be sure you understand what the actual work is that you'll be doing, and that you like it! ~ Monica, 47, instructional designer, Chicago, IL

Make sure you like the work, because performance is the only criteria you're measured by. ~ Sam, 62, computer programmer working in the transportation industry, Portland, OR

Design your offer carefully and precisely with specific targets for income, profit, work schedule in mind so that you can remain in control of where being independent leads. If you aren't working your own plan, you'll be working someone else's. ~ Theo, 50, performance consultant, Chicago, IL

To become independent, one should really be an expert or specialized in something. Once you are independent, you are alone and on your own to sell yourself or your expertise. ~ Jaakko, 53, chemical industry technology consultant, Istanbul, Turkey

Take a look at your closest competitor. Make sure you have a niche you're fulfilling in the market. ~ Rachelle, 51, Montessori educator, Seattle, WA

Have you run the numbers?

Reflecting on the start of my own journey as an independent, I can say that hands down, the question about whether or not I could make enough money was my biggest fear as I contemplated making the leap. I'd watched my own entrepreneurial father go from boom to bust over the first fourteen years of my life. Watching the family business fail was not fun, and I sure as heck did not want to inflict that pain upon myself.

I have heard some people suggest that you should take your current full-time income before taxes and multiply it by three to get to the number to get to the total revenue dollars you need to make as an independent. However, that might be very unhelpful advice depending on your circumstances. If I would have taken that advice, I would still be sitting in a cube farm because there is *no way* I would ever be able to triple the amount I was making when I stopped working full time. Below is the process I used to figure out the numbers.

In order to break through the fear, I spent a lot of time and energy running the numbers. I set up three spreadsheets that represented three personal budgets. I recommend this exercise to anyone considering making the leap and urge anyone who does it to be brutally realistic.

Step 1: Set up the spreadsheets

A. DireStraits.xls: This is literally the budget for survival. Include the bare amount of money you need in order to keep a roof over your head, food in your belly, health insurance, transportation to get to your clients, and payments to keep the bill collectors at bay (i.e., student loan payment). Don't include anything for savings (for retirement or otherwise), money for eating out, or budget for fun things like movies, theater, travel, or gift giving. In a dire straits world, you can't do those sorts of things.

If you have a family, include the bare minimum for them: food in their bellies, health insurance, clothes on their back, and basic school fees. Don't include money for extracurricular activities or wants.

B. **MiddleOfTheRoad.xls:** Include everything from the DireStraits spreadsheet and add a few items. Include some money for retirement savings, emergency cash savings, one fun thing a week like seeing a movie or eating out, basic personal care needs like getting a professional haircut or a little new clothing, and modest gift giving for the most important people in your life.

If you have a family, include a line item for some college savings if that is a priority for your family. Add budget around high priority, but optional medical needs like braces. Add one extracurricular activity a month and a modest amount for new clothes and entertainment.

C. **HighOnTheHog.xls:** Include everything you need and want to live the life style you desire. Start with the MiddleOfTheRoad.xls and adjust the savings line to reflect your ideal level of savings. Perhaps add a line item for charitable giving. Increase the gift giving line item to include close friends. Consider your personal care desires: add things like gym membership, monthly manicures, quarterly facials, and massages. Add budget for purchasing a new car and taking a great vacation.

If you have a family, increase the level of college savings to your ideal amount. Do the same for extra-curricular activities and things like summer camp. If you have a new driver in the family and want to add a car to the family, include those dollars.

Step 2: Consider what you think you can realistically make

A. **Determine how many weeks in the year you are going to work.** My first year, I assumed I would take two weeks off for holidays and an extra two weeks for vacation and/or sick time. In this example, that equals 48 working weeks.

B. **Determine how many hours a week you think you can realistically work.** By realistic, I mean how many hours a week can you work *without* other areas of your life breaking down. For me, I knew going into my independent life that I could realistically work 40-45 hours. What was true then, and still applies today, is that when I work more than 45 hours a week, I am not cooking enough meals at home, keeping my home neat and tidy, seeing friends regularly, and getting to the gym. And when those things don't happen, I get very crabby and become extremely ineffective.

C. **Determine how many of those weekly hours can be billable.** The need to be realistic continues. Of course, you'd like to think that every moment of your working time is going to be billable (meaning the time you are working can be billed back to a client), but the reality is that you will have a lot of non-billable tasks to complete in order to keep the trains running on time. *And,* I recommend you be conservative about how much work you are going to be able to drum up in your first year. My first year, I assumed I could keep myself billable 30 hours a week. If that number seems too high for yourself, lower it to 20 or 25.

D. **Determine your hourly rate. Again, it pays to be realistic here.** It's likely that there is a range for what people who do what you do make. For this exercise, you should be conservative. Assume the lower end of the range (However, you should ask for their higher end of your range when you actually sell your time to your clients!). My number when I did this exercise was $75/hour—worth noting... I've made more than that per hour on every project I've ever worked on in ten years.

How do you figure out your rate?

One way is to take your current full-time salary, plus benefits and divide it by 2,080 (52 weeks a year, multiplied by 40 hours). Or ask trusted colleagues who are independents about their rates. Some independents don't feel comfortable being 100% open about their rates—especially if you are going to end up being their competition. The best way to broach this subject is to say something like, "This is the rate I am thinking about charging for this specific type of work. What do you think?" If the person is a trusted colleague, she will tell you if she thinks you are too high or too low.

A. **Calculate your possible realistic income.**
- Weeks Worked x Billable Hours = Total Number of Annual Billable Hours
- Total Billable Hours x Hourly Rate = Gross Income
- For me it looked like this:
  48 Weeks x 30 Billable Hours = 1,440 Annual Billable Hours
  1,440 x $75 = $108,000 (my estimated gross income)

B. **Subtract taxes.** This is a painful reality for us independents. It's highly recommended that (in the United States) you plan for 40% of your income to go toward taxes. I do this and have never not been able to pay my taxes. And, most years I end up having a few thousand extra dollars sitting in my tax account. This becomes a nice little bonus!

C. **Subtract business expenses.** This is different for different people, but things like accountant fees, office supplies, and business insurance (if needed). In my first year, I did not need business insurance and I was working from my dining room table so my overhead costs were pretty low. I conservatively budgeted $2,500.

D. **Determine your take home income.**
- Gross Income x .60 (remember, 40% is going for taxes) = Income After Taxes
- Income After Taxes – Business Expenses = Total Net Income
- For me it looked like this:
  $108,000 x .60 = $64,800 - $2,500 = $62,300 (my net income)

Step 3: Compare the numbers

Look at your three budget worksheets from step 1. How do those total numbers compare with the realistic net income amount in step 2?

- If your net income is higher than all three budget numbers (and you were brutally realistic with your assumptions to get that number), then this is a very good day for you! Find your first couple of clients and get going.

- If your net income is higher than your MiddleOfTheRoad and your DireStraits numbers, I'd still argue this is a good day because remember, you were being realistic and conservative (you were, weren't you?). It's likely that you'll beat your projections and as your business grows, it's a safe bet that your income picture will only get better.

- If your net income is just at or below your DireStraits number, you should think very long and hard about whether the business you want to go into is the right financial move. It might mean that in order to make it work, you'll need to work way more hours than is healthy for you. And... even if *you* are willing to work more hours, you have to consider if you can drum up enough business to make all those hours billable—especially as you start out. Taking a moonlighting approach to getting started might be a safer approach.

This exercise was enlightening to me because my DireStraits number was $38,000. Meaning, it was imperative that I make at least that amount to eat and keep a roof over my head. But remember, after I ran the step two numbers, I figured out that I was likely going to net $62,300. That was $24,300 of "head room" above my DireStraits number. So, even if my assumptions—which were already conservative—didn't come to fruition, I'd still be okay. And, I had three months of emergency cash in the bank, which gave me a little more sense of security as I jumped off the ledge.

This is a cautionary tale, my friends. You might be wondering how it worked out for me my first year. Honestly, it wasn't as great as I'd hoped... I grossed $93,000, which was $15,000 less than I thought I would do in my first year (remember, I estimated I would make $108,000). This is why I can't stress enough how important it is to be realistic and conservative. I thought I was being just that, and I *still* wasn't as billable as I thought I would be in my first year. But it wasn't tragic, because I was still $9,300 above my DireStraits number and I did what I needed to do to make it through the first year. And make it, I did. By my second year, I grossed $151,000 and have never looked back.

Once you determine that you have the right stuff, have a solid handle on what it is you are going to offer the world, know that people are willing to pay you for it, and have pushed on the numbers in a realistic and conservative way and have proven (for your own comfort level) that you can make it work, it's time to get the wheels in motion. Read on, my intrepid friend! There is much work to begin.

Chapter
Four

Making the Leap:

*How to Plan your
Transition*

Alan Lakin, best-selling time management author, said, "Planning is bringing the future into the present so that you can do something about it now." It's a simple sentence, but it's packed full of wisdom. There is no doubt about it, becoming an independent is a BIG change, and with any change or transition, it's best to have a plan.

The process of becoming an independent consultant is a lot like the process of moving to a new city. If you've ever had this wonderful life experience, I bet you had a plan. You had to figure out where you were going, share your plan with others, set a timeline, gather the supplies, get other human beings lined up to help (thanks, Dad!), take care of administrative tasks like turning on/off utilities, pack, and at least a hundred other things to make your move happen.

There are also things that are nice to do, but you may not have time. For example, how many times in the lead up to a move have you thought, "I am going to go through all my stuff and purge before the movers come."

And, how many times have you actually done that? I know for me, I have moved several boxes marked "grad school stuff" five times. I'm guessing if I walked down to the basement right now and looked in those boxes, there is nothing worth saving. But, the reality is, in a time of big change or transition when there are so many things to do, some of the unnecessary stuff falls off the to-do list. And while it would be nice if you could do everything on your list, it is actually a good thing to be able to prioritize— you are already putting your action-orientation and organization skills to work!

Transitioning into the gig economy is actually a lot like moving...

Figure out where you are going

Check! You did that in the last chapter. But in case you are skipping around (which is totally legit), it's critically important to articulate in a clear and concise way, what it is that you have to offer the world. Consider going back to the end of the last chapter to see examples of how I articulate what my business offers the world.

Share your plan with others

There are two different sets of people you should start sharing with—your inner circle, or as I call my people, "Team Gretchen." And, professional colleagues (maybe).

Just like during the lead up to a move, if you live with anyone, you have to get them on board with the idea of moving and you need their agreement to go with you. Same deal here. If you have a spouse or partner, it's best to include them early in your planning and make sure they understand, and are comfortable with what your plan looks like physically, emotionally, and financially. I'm no couple's therapist, but I am assuming that making the move to the gig economy will be smoother—especially in the harder moments—when your partner is supportive.

You might also consider sharing your plans with your children, if it applies. While kids likely won't have much of a vote about where you take your career, it's a pretty safe bet that they will be impacted—especially if you are working from home.

I know several independents who have created specific norms in their households about when the kids can have access to Mom/Dad and when they need to take care of themselves (or rely on a hired child care provider in the house). And, if you are anticipating that money might be tighter than normal in the first 12-18 months, it's probably worth a family conversation about what that might mean for everyone.

Your early idea of joining the gig economy is fragile—handle with care! It's possible you have all kinds of tapes running through your brain driven by fears and self-doubt—I know I did in the beginning. It's not uncommon for people to project their own fears and self-doubts onto you if you find yourself sharing your plans. Being exposed to these conversations can amplify, and possibly distort your own feelings—making those fears sound very loud.

With that said, I am not suggesting you only share with people who are going to blindly encourage you. It's a fabulous idea to discuss your plans with trusted dear ones who will ask smart questions to deepen your thinking. In fact, you should totally do that! I am simply suggesting that you be selective.

On the professional side of things, I found it useful to reach out to some established independents in my field, who were also trusted colleagues and friends. It was a boost to my spirit to hear "atta girls" and enthusiastic encouragement from people who knew me professionally and were doing the work I wanted to do. They were able to give me solid input about why they thought I would be successful as an independent and share their lessons learned. Their specific encouragement helped push me over the hump to walk in and submit my resignation.

And, no matter what your timeline is for making the leap... amp up your networking game. Now. Stop reading. Go network! Seriously, it is imperative that you start laying the groundwork because most independents will tell you, it is from your network that most of your business will come. Let me say that again... IT IS FROM YOUR NETWORKS THAT MOST OF YOUR BUSINESS WILL COME.

If you've been working in the comfy confines of your cube or office walls, it's time to start getting visible. And it's much better to announce to a network that is already warmed up that you are going to become an independent, then it is to ask people for things who have barely heard from you in months or years. Remember, one of the characteristics of a successful independent is to be authentic. And, asking people for help who haven't heard from you in a long time is not authentic.

One thing I wish I would have known when I first struck out on my own is that it really would work out. That good planning and a great network make all the difference. ~ Isabelle, 44, writer and editor, Chicago, IL

Build a solid network first. Give to your network more than you get, and you'll find you will never be out of work. You should reach out to your network three times more to help with something than you do to ask for help. ~ Hannah, 49, business consultant working in the healthcare industry, Bourbonnais, IL

Network like crazy!!! ~ Tom, 58, graphic designer working in the branding/marketing industry, Boulder, CO

Networking is so important. Every person you meet could potentially lead to work, so treat EVERYONE that way. ~ Sylvie, 47, management consultant, Knoxville, TN

I was surprised by how easily I have found work—mostly through my network. ~ Sid, 30, freelance writer and communications specialist, Auckland, New Zealand

If you are in a situation where you don't have a long runway before you strike out on your own, that's fine. Use whatever time available to start networking. Write LinkedIn recommendations for people you've valued working with, send an article that you really know will resonate with a colleague based on what they are working on and thinking about these days, attend some industry events, join your local chamber of commerce. Go. Don't delay!

- Watch Heather White's TedTalk, *It's Not About Working the Room*
- Read Keith Ferrazzi and Tahl Raz's *Never Eat Alone: And Other Secrets to Success, One Relationship at a Time*
- Read Casciaro, Gino, and Kouchaki's *Harvard Business Review article, Learn to Love Networking*

Set a timeline

Do you have a move date? If you have the luxury of planning ahead, this section is for you. Identify the critical path tasks that need to be completed before you take the leap and do those things first. For example, if you are leaving a job that provides health insurance, schedule all your appointments—get a physical, get a mammogram, take your kids in for dental cleanings, use all your flexible spending account (FSA) money.

I've mentioned it before, but it bears repeating... have enough cash for three-to-six months of living expenses in the bank. If possible, pay down debt. In your first few lean months (and really anytime) it's nice to have fewer bills to pay.

If possible, wrap up critical path projects at your current job or identify recommendations for how the work can get transferred to others. This might not always be possible, but it's best not to leave your current employer in the lurch. First, it's not cool. Second, they could very well become a future source of income—but there is no way that is happening if you burn the bridge.

Then, set the date. And this is key... don't move it (unless you have a *really good* reason). The reality is that there is never a perfect moment. There will always be one more project to wrap up, one more connection to make, one more dollar to save. Personally, I took four months from the moment I decided to go out on my own to actually quit my full-time job. This was my timeline because there was lots to do. Read on...

Gather the supplies

Just like with moving, you have to gather your supplies. Here's what I gathered for my business:

Equipment/hardware

- Laptop
- A second monitor

- Scanner
- Printer
- Back-up hard drive or online backup service (with no I.T. department, it's important to have a plan in place to make sure you are protecting your work)
- Cell phone
- Office furniture

Software

- Microsoft Office
- Project management software (e.g., Microsoft Project™ or Smartsheets™)
- Accounting software (e.g., Quicken™, QuickBooks™)
- File sharing (e.g., Dropbox™, Google Drive™, SharePoint®, Basecamp™)
- Video/web conferencing (e.g., Zoom™, Webex™, GoTo Meeting™)
- Website hosting company

Marketing

- Logo
- Website (URL, hosting, design)
- Business email address (even if it is just a separate Gmail™ account)
- Business cards

For most independents, getting a website and your branding perfected is not the highest priority as you get started. Honestly, you can start working without any of that in place and you might not ever need it. Conversely, I have seen many people burn weeks or months getting their new branding just right. Take care to not let this part of starting your own business become an excuse to not get going.

As Hannah, a business consultant working in the healthcare industry said when asked what she wish she would have known when she struck out on her own, "You don't need a fancy website. You don't need expensive brochures. What you do need is a strong, diverse network. Focus on relationships. Find ways every week to help others in your field, and it will come back to you time and time again."

Other

- Office supplies (I regularly use printer paper, ink, and envelopes)
- Postage

Establish your space

You need a place to put your stuff and, most importantly, do the work. The environment in which humans are most productive is incredibly personal. Some people do better with a little background noise, while others need absolute quiet. Some people spend many hours on conference calls, so need a quiet space to work where there won't be background noise and where they won't distract others with their conversation. While others have active households and need a way to set boundaries about their availability to the people in their household.

Here are things that I've found useful over the years:

- **Dedicated space.** I like having space to have temporary piles for my active projects. So, I need to have a space where I can have a few piles and not feel like I have to move them every day. As such, I need a dedicated desk that is 100% (or at least almost) dedicated to my work space. For seven years, I worked from my dining room table. I lived alone so this didn't bother anyone, but I had to move my piles a few times a year when hosting guests or a dinner party. Three years ago, I finally just converted my dining room into an office (And now when people come for dinner, we eat on our laps!).

- **Peace and quiet.** I like limited background noise and because I spend at least a few hours a day on the phone, I need a quiet environment. Therefore, I work from my home office most of the time. Occasionally, I'll pack up my laptop and head to the local coffee shop if I need a change of pace.

- **Pet management.** Fortunately, my dog is pretty quiet. He has a dog bed in my office and pretty much hangs out there while I am working. He does, however, have moments when he gets restless. I keep his leash handy and if he starts barking or getting generally annoying, I put his leash on and use a technique called "tethering" where I tie him to my leg—we've been doing this since he was a puppy and he knows it means, "Dude, be quiet. Mommy is working."

I know other independents who close their animals out of their offices when they are on calls. While clients these days are used to working with people who work from home (and may also do so), it is unprofessional to consistently have barking dogs in the background.

- **Family management.** Admittedly, I do not have children, so this one is pretty easy for me. But like pet noise, you need to have a strategy for children noise. The occasional interruption is not a big deal, but consistent family background noise is unprofessional. However, I work with many fellow independents who work from home and have children. Here are some strategies they use:
  - One colleague has a hard and fast rule with her family that when

her office door is closed, that means she is not at home—she's at the office. She hires a baby sitter to be in the house while she is working and unless someone is bleeding, she is not available.

- Another colleague with younger children sets her work schedule and expectations with her clients to only work when her kids are at day care or school. And, in the situations when the kids are home, she tells clients when she agrees to meet with them outside her regular work hours that her kids will be home and there might be some background noise.

- **Coworking space.** Some people find working in a coworking space effective. They like having a place to go every day or a few days a week. And, they like having a community and access to shared services like printers and use of conference rooms. I've explored the possibility and think it would be useful if I had less control over my space (i.e., if I lived with anyone) or if I was new to a city and wanted to feel less isolated. But, as it stands, I haven't wanted to incur the expense of renting a co-working space.

- **Ergonomics.** It's important to honor your body and make sure you are not causing injury. For me this means a really good chair, a foot pedestal, and if I am typing a lot, I switch from typing on my laptop keyboard to using an ergonomic keyboard and mouse. Listen to your body and if anything is feeling cranky, don't let it hurt for too long. Consider hiring an occupational therapist or ergonomics specialist to assess your space and make suggestions. I am personally considering investing in a stand up desk that would allow me to sit or stand.

- **Consider placement.** I like lots of sunlight and fresh air in the summer so like having windows. However, I don't like facing outside because I am easily distracted by the activity on my busy street. Also, I have several clients I meet with on video conference so I'm cognizant of what's behind me and in frame on my camera.

Get other human beings lined up

As in moving, you might engage a realtor, hire a decorator, find a contractor to complete pre-move in preparations, and then hire movers. Making the leap to your independent life requires the same sort of thing. I'll cover more about this in Chapter 5: Building Your Team, but here are some of the key people you should consider lining up:

- Your first client

- Accountant

- Attorney

- A couple trusted colleagues you can call with questions

Take care of administrative tasks

For me, this is the hardest part about moving—signing the lease of mortgage, dealing with the utilities at the old and new place, cleaning the new place and tracking back to clean the old place, and on and on...

This is also my least favorite part of being an independent. And like dealing with the minutiae of day-to-day life, these tasks are relentless. And they must be done! Here's a list of things I recommend based on my own journey:

- Apply to become a Limited Liability Company (LLC) (or incorporate in whatever way you and your accountant deem necessary)

- Learn how to use your accounting software

- Secure health insurance

- Secure business insurance (if necessary)

- Set up a business bank account(s)

- Secure a business credit card

- Set up your work space
- Draft your boiler plate contract (and have an attorney look at it)
- Clean up your social media (Have you said controversial things on Twitter™ that might not align with the people who are going to hire you? Consider taking those down.)

Move

All your thinking and planning is done (for now). It's time, make the move. Take the leap!

One thing I wish I would have known when I started is that it always works out. ~ Abigail, 47, learning strategy consultant, Evanston, IL

Jump. With both feet at once. Do it! ~ Meredith, 39, sales and marketing consultant in the educational product industry, Granger, IN

I was so scared to leave my corporate job, but what a blessing it has been. It's stretched me in so many ways. ~ Tyler, 48, founder of a marketing research firm, Atlanta, GA

I was surprised that being an independent is not the "fly by the seat of your pants" existence that I expected. ~ Max, 46, voiceover artist, Asheville, NC

Go for it. ~ Sally, 65, management consultant, Milwaukee, WI

It's way more fun than I expected. It's tons of work, but it's so much fun to escape the grind of the institutional environment. ~ Gerry, 61, founder of a healthcare startup, Atlanta, GA

Make sure you have a foundational client while you build. Just get to work. Stop swirling in websites, etc. WORK! That stuff will come. Know that your business will change and evolve over time—so just get started. ~ Maya, 37, a strategic communications consultant, Atlanta, GA

Just do it now! There's no right time to start. So, start right this minute. ~ Judy, 53, wellness and travel industry freelance writer, San Francisco, CA

Go for it, you only learn through the action. You can prepare as much as you like, but the best learning comes from doing. ~ Vanessa, 40, AgriTech consultant, New Zealand.

Chapter Five

Building Your Team:

Being an Independent Doesn't Mean Working Alone

Being an independent does not mean you work alone, it really just means that you work with others in a different way. Exactly who you need to put around you is somewhat dependent on the work you do. And, I've found that my team needs to include both professional and personal resources in a way that is very different from my days of working in a full-time job.

For example, when I was a full-time employee, I viewed having a cleaning service to clean my condo as a luxury or a nice treat to give myself (and there is nothing wrong with that if you can afford it!). As an independent, I view those two and half hours that two people spend cleaning my home as a way to free up more billable time—it would take me at least five hours to do what they do and my home would not be nearly as clean! And, the fact that I don't have to spend hours on the weekend cleaning, means I can use that time to rest and recharge—which is critical to my success.

Now, did I hire a cleaning service my first week as an independent? No. In the first lean months, I did almost everything myself and managed my budget closely. But, as my business grew (and continues to grow), the composition of the team around me changes.

In fact, it ebbs and flows throughout the year and from year-to-year based on how much opportunity is surfacing and how much I choose to work. As I type, I have nineteen fellow independent contractors working with me. Some years, I've had zero. It's partly driven by the marketplace—which has had a lot of need over the last eighteen months. And it's in part driven by my choices. First, I am choosing to have a lot of plates spinning this year. Second, I set a goal to write this book, which means that I need time—enter outsourcing some project work to others. The subtext here is that when you are an independent, you get to choose and you get to keep choosing.

Here's my two cents of the sorts of people you might consider having on your team, and the point(s) at which you might need to tap into them. I've outlined the list based on my own experience and am quite sure this looks different, for different people and in different industries. For instance, this list would look different if you are in a highly regulated industry—you would likely need way more legal input coming from your team. This is what worked for me, as a new independent consultant.

Accountant

When to identify: Right away

How they can help you:

- Gives advice on how to initially structure your company. Should you become an LLC? Should you incorporate? What are the tax implications of these different choices?
- Tells you how to register with the state or can do it for you.
- Explains the ins and outs of paying quarterly taxes. How much should you pay to the state and to the federal government each quarter to avoid penalties? By when to pay? How to actually make the payments? (My accountant calls me each quarter to remind me to pay.)
- Provides suggestions on how to set up your Chart of Accounts in your accounting software and what you can and can't write off as business expenses
- Informs you about what paperwork you need to hold on to and for how long
- Recommends how to pay yourself a salary and year-end bonuses
- Suggests how and when you should make payments into your retirement accounts so that you are leveraging the tax code to your benefit

- If you engage fellow sub-contractors, helps you navigate how to pay them and report their earnings to the government.
- Answers questions about how to respond when you get random (at least it feels random) requests from the government to file this form or that form. In my experience, this happens about every other year.
- Prepares your taxes (You thought that was going to be the only bullet point, huh?)
- Provides critical advice about how to avoid getting flagged by the IRS when you file your taxes
- Helps you navigate an audit should you find yourself in that situation

Things to consider:

- Ask fellow independents for referrals, how they utilize their accountants, and roughly, how much they pay annually
- Interview a few candidates. Make sure you like this person and that you share a similar communication style. It is time consuming to switch to another accountant down the road, so it's worth investing the time up front to find the right person.
- Rates
- From my personal experience, it is useful to work with an accountant who has a cadre of independents as clients as we have different needs than larger entities. If you are not a finance guru, you need someone who is patient and willing to answer basic questions (over and over), will hold your hand through the process, and can anticipate what you don't know in order to keep you out of hot water with the IRS.
- My accountant is also an attorney, which has come in handy over the years. It's nice that I can go to one person who knows my business to talk about multiple things. And, because he has a duel expertise, he is often thinking with both parts of his brain when we are working

through any given situation.

Find a great accountant. I mean really good. Take the time to talk to them and check references. It's so hard to break up with them once you've been with them. ~ Abigail, 47, learning strategy consultant, Evanston, IL

Keep good records. Get a good accountant. Don't be tempted to do things that get you audited. I've seen people get audited and it's not pretty. ~ Max, 46, voiceover artist, Asheville, NC

I wish I would have known in the beginning that you should not do everything on your own—like financial stuff and taxes. In the beginning, there is not yet money, so you think doing everything yourself is needed. Don't think that. ~ Yara, 38, marketing consultant, The Hague, Netherlands

My advice is to invest in the beginning in people who can help with the financial end of the business—I have seen the value in having that help sooner rather than later. ~ Leslie, 45, agent/advocate/promoter supporting authors and speakers, Atlanta, GA

Trusted advisors

When to identify: Right away

How they can help you:

- Provides thought partnership and advice on how to handle specific situations
- Answers a myriad of tactical questions about running your own

consulting practice

- Provides, at times, social interaction. Have a group of fellow independents you can reach out to for a quick conversation can help guard against isolation.
- Joins you on projects once your plate gets too full
- Refers business your way when their plates get too full

Things to consider:

- Identify a few fellow independents who work or live near you so that you have easy, go-to people to grab lunch with.
- Consider joining a formal advisory group like Vistage® International. Or, hire a business coach (I'm available to coach...). Personally, I joined Vistage® for the first three years of my business and found it incredibly useful and worth the investment. I was confident about doing the actual consulting work, but had a lot to learn about actually running a business—which is what you are doing when you become an independent.
- Check out Meetup.com to see if there are any small business groups who meet in your area.

Ask for help, delegate if you can, work on a team—even if it is a team of independents. ~ Frank, 59, realtor, Milwaukee, WI

I wish I would have understood from the beginning that you need to be an "all rounder" and learn how to run a business, not just be good at the service you offer. ~ Olivia, 42, human resources consultant, Boston, MA

Align yourself with great talent that compensates for your weaknesses. ~ Sylvie, 47, management consultant, Knoxville, TN

I was surprised that there was such a thriving community of people just like me, where I could get ideas and advice. ~ Jennifer, 29, freelance copywriter, Alberta, Canada

I wish I would have known sooner that I may be on my own, but I don't have to go it alone. Find the resources that truly help and support—they're out there! ~ Judy, 46, voice over actress, Washington, DC

Know that you are not alone and find your tribe of folks to support and encourage you on your journey. Having a network of people to lean on is so important. ~ Diane, 49, landscape and wildlife photographer, Chicago, IL

Know the holes in your knowledge and train up. Speak to as many people as possible who have done what you want to do. ~ Olivia, 42, human resources consultant, Boston, MA

Attorney

When to identify: It depends.

I am not an attorney. When and how you use an attorney is dictated by the nature of your business. What follows is my personal experience and shall not be construed as legal advice (My attorney told me to say that). Fortunately, my work is fairly straightforward so I have not had to utilize the services of an attorney too much.

How they can help you:

- Sets up boilerplate language for your standard contracts. In my business, the contracts I use the most are proposals to clients and contracts with fellow independents who are joining my project.

- Reviews contracts. In my business, many clients ask me to sign non-disclosure agreements and/or master services agreements. Early on, I had no idea what I was looking at so it was useful to have an attorney. Ten years in, I rely on my attorney less and less for this sort of thing.
- Assists in navigating intellectual property questions

Things to consider:

- Rates and how they bill (by the hour, quarter hour, etc.)
- Work with an attorney who is used to working with independent consultants

Technical support

When to identify: Early on.

Having an IT department to call when something is not working is the thing I miss the most about working in a full-time job.

How they can help you:

- Recommends what hardware to purchase
- Sets up stable and robust Wi-Fi. Do you want to be able work from every room in your house?
- Trouble shoots technical issues
- Suggests a process for backing up and archiving digital files

Things to consider:

- Fortunately, I work in the technology world and hire graphic designers and developers to join my projects. So, it is fairly easy for me to find someone with technical chops and who have a vested interest in keeping my business up and running. Leverage your network.

- I made a strategic decision to conduct my day-to-day work from a Mac because it's a more stable operating system—which means less possibility of bugs and viruses. Therefore, I have few tech support needs. Note, I have no issues passing files back and forth with my clients, 99% of whom work in a Windows environment. I did purchase a PC so that I can test programs in an environment more like my client's—but that is very specific to the industry I am in. I use that PC about ten times a year.

- The other nice thing about working on a Mac is that it is very easy for me to make an appointment at Genius Bar™ at the Apple® Store and get technical support that way.

Graphic designer

When to identify: This is somewhat dependent on your business, but for the typical business consultant, you should consider identifying this person in the first 6-12 months.

How they can help you:

- Designs your branding (logo, business cards, contract template, invoice template, PPT template)

- Designs and develops your website and other marketing collateral

- Adds polish to client deliverables, as needed

Things to consider:

- If you read the advice from the trenches above, you can see the overwhelming recommendation is to just get started. Don't let establishing your branding stand in the way of making the leap. That is sound advice.

- Check out Fiverr.com. You can post your project and your budget. Different freelancers bid on your project and share samples of their work.

- Look at the level of polish presented by your competitors and make sure your branding matches or exceeds that level. It's better to have nothing at all, then to have something that looks unprofessional.

Financial advisor

When to identify: Sometime in the first six months—once the money starts rolling in!

How they can help you:

- Determines the best strategy for retirement savings. This is critical as you no longer have a company-sponsored 401K. There are good options for independents and a financial advisor can help you understand your options.

- Makes investment recommendations.

- In addition to your accountant, a financial advisor helps you do yearly tax planning with an investment lens.

Things to consider:

- I work with a fee-only advisor who has a fiduciary responsibility to act in my best interest. She does not accept any fees or compensation based on product sales. I pay her a flat fee to do a big plan for me every few years and a smaller flat fee to rebalance my portfolio on an annual basis.

- You can also find good financial advisors with retail financial services firms like Fidelity® or Edward Jones®, to name just a couple. You should get referrals and interview a few advisors. Once you start working with someone, it can be time consuming to move the relationship elsewhere.

Personal support team

When to identify: Anytime you need it, and start sooner rather than later

How they can help you:

- Takes some of the administrative load off your plate in order to allow you to focus on more profitable activity
- Provides emotional support
- Enables you to manage your energy so you stay healthy and balanced

Here are some of the people on my personal support team:

- My dog, Ocho. He gets me up out of my chair and moving around a few times a day. Plus, he makes a great foot warmer under my desk!
- My friends. A lot of these people are also trusted advisors. But it's important to understand the distinction between when you are reaching out to a colleague for advice about a business situation and when you just need a friend with whom to laugh and play. Both are important! And for me, I try to keep it very clear. When I am working, I am working. When I am resting and playing, I am resting and playing.
- Cleaning service. They come every five to six weeks and do a deep clean of my entire home. Check with your accountant to see if you can write off a percentage of this cost.
- Doggy Day Care. Ocho goes to day care a few times a week when I am in a particularly busy period of time. This alleviates the guilt I feel that he's not getting much interaction.

- Hourly admin support. I've used TaskRabbits™ over the years to act as a personal assistant doing everything from entering receipts into QuickBooks™, taking Ocho to the groomer, grocery shopping, scanning documents, and even taking down my Christmas tree.

As an independent, I like to use on-demand services rather than hire an employee. The nature of my work ebbs and flows and while there are times when I am really busy, there are other times when I choose to slow down. I personally like the flexibility to scale up or down without having to manage someone's productivity.

However, when I start to feel overwhelmed, that is when I start a TaskRabbit™ list. Once I have about a day's worth of tasks on the list, I make an appointment and hire someone to come in and help. I've had periods of time where I do this every three to four weeks.

No matter how hard you plan, you are in for some surprises. Make sure you have good friends to keep you sane and on track! ~ Andrew, 55, debt review practitioner, Cape Town, South Africa

Hire people to do the things you are not good at, that makes you nervous, or that drains your energy. Your time is valuable and it will only be considered as such, if you consider it as valuable first! ~ Bridget, 48, addiction recovery counselor, Northern Virginia

Chapter Six

Making it Work:

*Finding Clients and
Landing Business*

"How do you find your clients?" It's the question I get asked more than any other. It's a fair and important question.

As mentioned repeatedly throughout this book, your network is going to be your best resource for generating new business. In the first six months in business as an independent consultant, I did projects with two past employers—a good argument for never burning your bridges! And, those relationships continue to generate business today.

What's more, many of my clients today were once on project teams at previous clients from five years ago. They left their original companies and took new positions—usually with more decision-making authority—and because of their experience working with me at the first company, they bring me on to do projects at their new company. And just like that, my client list has grown.

I've also, over the years, attended conferences and simply started conversations with people where I ask them questions about what they do and I share a bit about the work my company does. After the conference, I make sure I connect with those folks on LinkedIn and then more often than not, people with whom I made a true connection, usually end up surfacing at some point asking if I have time to take on a new project. I liken it to planting a garden. You plant the seeds and wait for them to grow. Some of the seeds may never sprout, some might get carried off by birds, and others grow into a bountiful crop. Just keep planting!

The keys for me are: first, have truly authentic conversations and, second, make sure you are not in a position where you feel like you have to sell. If you are feeling desperate "to get business" and are in sales mode, then authenticity tends to fly out the window. If you are feeling desperate, then it's easy to fall into the trap of rushing a sale. No one likes to feel rushed. Consulting, no matter what your expertise, is about relationship building. You've got to build rapport with people so that when they do have a need, they will be open to hearing from you—and better yet, will simply reach out to ask you for help.

When I struck out on my own, I wish I would have known that the marketing never ends and most of the work comes from relationships. Cold calls don't work. ~ Kate, 63, graphic designer, Dallas, TX

I wish I had better understood how important networking is throughout your career to the success of being an independent. ~ Brad, 55, service design consultant, San Francisco, CA

Be flexible and open to the route you take to get to your destination. The oddest turns and connections often are the ones that lead to something special. ~ Jake, 50, leadership and business coach, Denver, CO

You will be helped spontaneously by others to build your business when you are eager to help them solve their problems first. ~ Stan, healthcare consultant, The Netherlands

So, how does one not feel desperate? As your business grows, this problem takes care of itself. The easiest way to not be desperate for work is to have plenty of it. But, as you build your business in the early days, my best advice is to live as lean as possible and have six months of cash saved. Typically, when people are "desperate for work," it's not because they are just dying to be working (Or, maybe that's just me. I'll be honest with anyone. I like what I do, but I would much rather be sailing). It's usually because they need money flowing in. The more you can do to minimize cash flow as an issue, the better.

Drumming up business

I am by no means a professional salesperson. In fact, I've been quite lucky throughout my career as an independent that I have not really had to sell in the traditional sense of the word. Meaning, I have not had to cold call. The closest I ever come to cold-calling is reaching out to my network to let them know I have some open capacity coming up. Usually, if I send an email like that, someone needs my services or knows someone who needs my services.

Having said that, I am aware of the different channels through which work comes my way. And, at any point in time, I can leverage these channels. It's probable that more than one of these is available to you regardless of your area of expertise. Here are the likely suspects for how you will find work. I've listed them in my preferred order, but the order for you will be dictated by your network and how much you want to hustle. My best advice is to cast your net wide.

Direct to you

Description: These are clients who contract directly with you or your company.

Pros:
- You have total control over the scoping of the project.
- You put all the profit generated by the project into your bank account.

- If it is a larger project that requires you to bring others on to do work, you control who joins the team.
- If you do good work and the client wants to continue working with you, then you reap the benefit of growing your own business.

Cons:

- The buck stops with you. Meaning, if you did not scope the project well or if things are going sideways on the project, it is you, my friend, that has to have those hard conversations with the client.
- You may have to navigate the vendor management process to become a preferred vendor partner in order to do work for the person who wants to hire you. This can be time consuming and can often require that you carry costly insurance.
- All back-office work falls to you including invoicing, collections, and paying taxes on the generated income.

Joining forces with a fellow independent

Description: These are projects that typically come through a fellow consultant with whom you've worked or who has worked with someone with whom you've worked. Their business model is usually such that they do not have full-time employees, but rather scale up their team based on their client's needs. In other instances, they may not have your expertise, but their project requires someone with your skillset.

Pros:

- You don't have to spend much time selling the work. Although sometimes a fellow independent may bring you in during the sales process to bolster the offering.
- Assuming you like and trust your fellow independent, you will likely

have a good experience for the duration of the project.

- Typically, a fellow independent is not going to take a huge chunk of money off each hour you work on the project, so these projects tend to be fairly profitable.

Cons:

- It is acceptable and should be expected that a fellow consultant hiring you to work on their project would ask you to sign a non-compete for a certain period of time for the client with whom you are working. But, this means that if further work comes from the project, whether or not you get to keep working for the client is completely at the discretion of the fellow consultant who owns the relationship. (And, if you are the consultant bringing others in on a project, you should have them sign non-competes.)

- Roles and responsibilities can be fuzzy in these sorts of engagements. Typically, when working with fellow independents, there is not a lot of established business process. We consultants are so busy working *in* our businesses that we rarely spend time working *on* our businesses. Because of this, it's important to make sure you have explicit conversations with potential partners so that expectations are clear from the start.

- You typically need to wait for them to get paid before you get paid.

Subcontracting through a larger company that provides the same services you provide

Description: In my industry there are several custom learning companies with thirty or more full-time employees who staff their projects first with their full-time employees, and then hire independent instructional designers and learning consultants to complete their project teams.

Pros:

- You don't have to spend time selling.

- Typically, your role on the project will be well defined and you'll be working on a team with established business processes (although there is no guarantee, so make sure you ask explicit questions and that all expectations are clearly documented in your contract).

- You usually do not have to interview with the client, rather the client fully trusts the company they hired to build a team that will fulfill on the work. The exception might be if you are going to step into a project management or highly strategic role. In these instances, the company might want to bring you in to meet the client stakeholders.

- Depending on your own network, you might have a chance to work with more highly strategic or big-brand companies than you could land on your own.

- Depending on the project, you might get exposure to new tools and business processes that you could use to augment the work you do with your own clients.

Cons:

- You will most certainly have to drop your rates as these companies tend to have higher overhead. In my experience, anywhere from 15-25%.

- Depending on your relationship with the company, you might find yourself working on projects that were scoped and sold by people you do not know and/or is being led by project managers with whom you've never worked. Therefore, they might have different standards about how a project should be managed. First, always begin such a project with explicit conversations about your role and the boundaries of your role before the project starts. If you don't discuss this beforehand, it is easy to get into a situation where you feel like you are being asked to leverage all your consulting skills, even though they are only explicitly paying for one specific part of your skill set.

- Project managers who primarily work with internal, full-time team members can often feel frustrated with you, a contract member of the team who is often hired only for part-time work, who predictably does not have as much flexibility (because you have commitments to other clients). Communication and up-front expectation setting are the keys to navigating these types of projects successfully.

Working through a staffing agency

Description: This relationship is fairly similar to working with a larger consulting firm that provides the same services, but with some marked differences. There are companies that are very transparent about being a staffing agency—companies like Manpower. And, there are other companies that position themselves in the marketplace as consulting firms. However, they have few, if any, full-time employees who are actually doing the work. What they do have, is a large sales force, recruiting team, and executive suite. More about that in a moment.

Pros:

- You don't have to spend time selling.
- Often, the staffing agency sends you to be interviewed by the client. So, in essence, you have the opportunity to sell yourself. While this is a hoop to jump through, it's also your chance to see if you like the client and to ask questions to determine if the project scope and timeline have been established in such a way that you think you can be

successful.

- You can count on getting paid regularly. Meaning, you don't have to wait for the staffing agency to collect from the client *before* you get paid.

- Many of these organizations provide support, coaching, sometimes project management, and input to the independents they place— which can be a huge benefit for newer consultants. Ultimately the relationship with the client is theirs, so they are invested in supporting you as you navigate sticky client situations.

- These companies tend to have a greater visibility in the marketplace because of larger marketing budgets so they get in the door at companies where you might not be able to by yourself.

Cons:

- You will likely have to drop your rates anywhere from 30-60%. Why so much, you might ask? These companies often have a large sales force, recruiting staff, executive suite, and marketing budget to support. That is a lot of overhead.

- You often have no control over the scope or timeline of the project. Usually, by the time the company is approaching you to join the project, it's been scoped and sold. This is not a big deal if the person selling the project is well versed in the work you do and realistic about how much time it takes. I mean WELL VERSED... Like they've sat in your seat and have done the work. However, if the sales team is disconnected from the actual work *and* the company does not have some checks and balances in place to make sure work is well-scoped, you can find yourself quite literally in the middle of a client service nightmare. Make sure you do your due diligence before you agree to join a project team.

- You may not know any of the people with whom you are working on the project. This could be fine, or could be an issue if you are stuck with underperformers.

- A lot of these projects tend to be onsite gigs. Meaning, the client wants you working in their office from 9-to-5. You have to decide if this is right for you. This is a con in my book (Literally. Ha!), as I treasure the time saved each day by having a short commute to my home office.
- You will likely be asked to sign a non-compete. That means, you cannot work directly with that client *and* you cannot work with that client through another consulting firm or agency.

It is completely fair and acceptable that company ask you to sign a non-complete. It is their relationship and it is in their best interest to protect that relationship. However, there are a few things to consider when you are the one being asked to sign.

If you decide to sign a non-compete agreement, you can negotiate some terms. For instance, the length of the agreement. From my perspective, anything longer than a year from the date of your final invoice seems excessive. Here's why: if you are taking a lower rate, then you should not *also* be allowing them to wrap you up for too long.

Let's say the staffing agency did a bad job scoping the project, therefore creating a situation where the project tanks and the client is unhappy. The client, understandably, makes the decision to not hire the staffing agency to fulfill future project work.

You are now in a situation where you can't work directly with the client (because of your non-compete agreement), you can't work for another agency who fulfills projects for that client (also because of your non-compete agreement), and you can't work with the client directly. Sounds like you got the short end of the stick.

Another term to consider in a non-compete is the "reach" of the agreement. I've had some agencies ask me to sign a non-compete for all clients in their portfolio. Um... no. I highly recommend you do not sign an agreement like this. You should only sign a non-compete for clients with whom you have direct contact. And, it should be *significant* direct contact. If you are taking on a small, short-term project, I recommend declining to sign or negotiate the terms to be much shorter in duration. For example, maybe only three to six months after the last invoice is submitted.

Is there ever a situation where you shouldn't sign? In my experience, there is only one situation where I have not been willing to sign. A staffing agency asked me to join a project where I already had an existing relationship with the client. In this instance, I only agreed to join the project with the agreement that I would not sign a non-compete. In addition, I was able to negotiate a higher rate because of my experience.

Sourcing projects through talent marketplaces

Description: These are platforms where you upload your resume and get matched with project-based opportunities. A few of the most popular are PwC's Talent Exchange™, MBO Connect®, Catalent®, and TalMix®.

Pros:
* If the marketplace is a good one, the projects are often with well-known companies with whom you might not otherwise have the

opportunity to work.

- In many cases, the client and the independent consultant can interact directly giving you more control over the scoping of the project.
- Because of the direct interaction, you have a little more room to negotiate rates.
- Some platforms act as the vendor through whom you work and take care of all the paperwork (i.e., contracting, invoicing, collections), relieving you of the need to go through the vendor management process which can be time consuming and can cost extra if they require you to carry specific insurance coverage.

Cons:

- The relationship is through a third party—albeit a technology platform, therefore you will likely have to drop your rates anywhere from 20-30%.
- Depending on your area of expertise, there may not be many opportunities. Different talent marketplace platforms specialize in different industries, so it might take some trial and error to find the one that works best for you.
- There are a lot of talent marketplaces like Fivvr® and UpWork® that specialize in low-cost project work. Beware of these sites—they are extremely transactional and treat talent more like commodities rather than experts. It's one thing to knock 20-30% off your rate. It's quite another to knock 80% off your rate. I'm an advocate for keeping your living expenses lean—especially as you get started. But I am not an advocate for undercutting your rates so much that you are not getting paid what you are worth. (Some will argue that this is great for the global economy and great for people getting started. These things are true, but neither have ever applied to me in my tenure as an independent.)

Is pro bono, bueno?

In short, it depends. I've seen new consultants take on pro bono projects in the hopes that a pro bono client will turn into a paying client. I'm not saying it will never happen, but don't count on it. There's a reason they aren't paying you, and it probably has something to do with not having much money. Unless there is something that is predictably going to change in the future, for example, they are a start-up about to receive their next cycle of investment dollars, it's likely they won't magically have money down the road.

If it's a situation where they want to "try you out..." Run, don't walk away. If they do not value the service and expertise you provide enough to pay you today, it's unlikely they will value it tomorrow.

All that said, taking a pro bono project makes a lot of sense if you are trying to sharpen a new skill or step outside your comfort zone or area of expertise. In that situation, by all means, work for free (or a deeply discounted rate). However, if you do this, be transparent about why you are saying yes to the work. First, to set the right expectation about your work and, second, so that after you gain the expertise, the client won't be surprised when you decline to take the next project for free.

It might also make sense to take on pro bono work for a cause that is near and dear to your heart. If you take this tack, be sure to clearly define the boundaries of your deliverables so that you don't get into a situation where the work never ends. In addition, before you say yes, make sure you have bandwidth. You don't want to put your paying projects at risk, and you don't want to disappoint the recipient of your good will.

While I do not consider myself a salesperson, the reality is that I am selling all of the time. I'm selling during conversations with colleagues, talking with current and former clients about possible projects, and by fulfilling my promises on the work my clients have entrusted to me and my team.

So, while this is not formal sales training, here are my tips for a non-sales salesperson:

1. **Understand your sales cycle.** You are not going to know this overnight, but in my line of business, I know that it takes about four-to-six weeks for a project to surface after I put an email out to my network or post something on LinkedIn indicating that I have open capacity. I also know that it takes about that amount of time to close a big project. So, I am always looking four-to-six weeks ahead to see if there is open space in my calendar. If there is, I know I need to get busy planting the seeds now so that work shows up.

2. **Have a system for tracking leads.** Mine is very low tech, but it works for my small business. I have a huge white board in my office and always keep a running list under the header, "leads." It's the list I turn to first when I see open space in my calendar and I know I need to start shaking the trees to find my next project. I also put reminders in my calendar to follow up with a prospect in an agreed upon timeframe.

3. **Establish a clear future**. This is sales speak for define the next step. For example, I had a prospect share that their company lost a big contract and while they want to start a project with me, they needed to wait until things settle down. I said, "I'm so sorry you are feeling the crunch. I know that is no fun. Thanks for sharing that with me and when you are ready, we are excited to get started. If you don't mind, I'll put a reminder in my calendar to reach out to you after the

holidays." She said, "Yes, I would appreciate that." When the time comes, it will make it much easier for me to reach out because we have an agreement.

4. **Stay in action.** Some people say that sales is a numbers game— meaning if you make enough calls, someone will say yes. I'm not so sure about that for the independent consultant. I think it's more of a prospecting and relationship game. If you do excellent work and nurture your network by staying in touch with people in meaningful ways then, when you have capacity, all you will have to do is let key people know you have time for a new project, and it's likely something will materialize. However, if you just go into a hole of work and don't stay in action around keeping your network fresh, when it comes time to say, "Hey guys, I'm available!" There might not be anyone around to hear you.

5. **Diversify.** Some consultants prefer to work full time on one client project at a time. And, they like it when one project rolls into the next project with that same client. While it is not my place to say this is a bad strategy, I will say that this strategy comes with some risks. Namely, if something happens unexpectedly to that project and it suddenly goes away... so does your cash flow. This may be okay if you have six months of emergency cash, but even with my emergency fund, I make decisions about what I am working on as though that emergency cash does not exist. I prefer to have a few projects going on at any one time with a few clients so that as timelines change or worse, a project abruptly ends, I can easily pivot into sales mode to fill the open capacity without feeling panicked.

Marketing your business

Just as I would never claim to be a sales person, I am also not a marketer.

Luckily, since I have no desire for world domination, I don't really need to spend much time on marketing. Do I have a logo? Yes. Do I have a website? Yes. Do I have a blog? Yes. Do I need any of this? It's questionable, and I did not need any of it in my first few years as an independent.

I have gotten exactly zero (you read that right... zero) clients or projects in ten years because they stumbled across my website. And, I have had work every day I wanted it since the day I hung out my shingle. So, while my website does not generate new leads, what it does do is provide a place for me to articulate my services and highlight my client list—helpful things when someone has been referred to me and wants to check me out.

I also write a couple blog posts a month, which forces me to pick my head up from the project work I am doing and think at a more meta level about the business of learning. The practice of writing these posts helps me work through and refine my own thinking about the industry I serve. Again, no one has ever called and said, "Hey, I read your blog post and I want to hire you." But, every time I post to my blog, I link to it from social media, which is a subtle way of reminding people, "Hey, Gretchen is out here and she's thinking about smart stuff."

Would I make any of this a high priority as you get started? Nope.

The art of saying no

There comes a time in almost every independent's life where they suddenly have too much work and face the tough task of saying no to work. This can be a real mind trip. Early in my tenure as an independent, I feared that if I said no, the client might never come back. Of course it's possible, but after ten years of experience I have two things to say about saying no.

First, if a client wants to hire you today, it is very unlikely that they are going to suddenly change their mind later and NOT want to work with you on a future project. This is not like dating. People generally don't feel rejected and angry because you said no—especially if you explain why. I've found that often clients are grateful that I know my limits and that I care enough about their project to not overcommit and then under deliver.

This leads me to my second point: while there is no guarantee that a client who you say no to will invite you to work for them in the future, it is a sure bet that if you under deliver and disappoint a client, they will not hire you again.

Here are some time-tested strategies for saying no gracefully:

1. You can say no to you *personally* doing the work, but see if you have a trusted fellow independent to whom you can subcontract the work. Frankly, this is how I inadvertently started to grow my business beyond being purely a one-woman show. This is a great solution if you trust your colleague to do the same caliber work you would do. And, if you have a little time to be a sounding board and review deliverables.

2. Explain that you do not have the capacity at the moment, but share with your client when you will be available. In my experience, clients can sometimes be willing to wait for a few weeks in order to have their first pick of partner.

3. Determine if there is a way to do a slow start so that it feels like the work is moving, but does not really ramp up until you have space in your calendar. In my experience, unless there is an absolutely unmovable date—which many are not really *that* unmovable—clients can find a way to make this work. Often, they just need to be able to

say, "we started this project" to their leadership.

4. If you cannot find a way to play any role in the project (see number one), then when you say no, it's a good practice to provide the client with the names and contact information for a few trusted fellow independents. That way, you are still providing them some sort of a solution to meet their need.

Chapter Seven

It's All in the Fine Print:

*Creating Solid
Agreements*

Congratulations, you have a client who wants to work with you! Be sure to pause and celebrate. Seriously. Not everyone gets to this point. It's something to feel good about. And now, it's time to create the agreement. One of the biggest lessons I've learned over the past decade is just how important it is to establish a clear agreement. If you do this well, it becomes the roadmap for the entire project.

Crafting a statement of work (SOW)

While the exact statement of work may vary from project-to-project, I find most agreements I craft have seven parts—and these are the actual headers I use in my agreements. Note, I am not an attorney and none of the language I share below should be assumed to be legal advice. As mentioned before, you should have an attorney review your contracts.

Project need

What it is: A one-to-two paragraph statement about what the client is inviting you to work on and why this work is important to their business.

Why it matters: This section serves three purposes:

1. I find writing this section is grounding exercise when I sit down to write an SOW. I often suffer anxiety and feel overwhelmed when faced with a blank page staring back at me. Getting this section written helps to kick-start the process.

2. It helps to ensure, right from the beginning, that you and the client agree about what the project is and why it's important.

3. I use the exact language in team and client kickoffs as a way to level set and start to articulate the edges of the scope sandbox.

Things to consider:

- **Keep it simple.** The client knows what the project is, so you don't need to write a soliloquy. If it's too long, the client might not read it, thus defeating the purpose to ensure alignment.

- **Focus on the ask.** What is it that they are asking you to do? Say it in plain, simple language.

- **Start defining the edges of the scope sandbox.** Have they already made decisions about what the solution should include? Have they already defined the audience? If so, include that detail.

- **State what the project is not.** This is not always needed, but if there is a clear "stopping point" or articulation of what the project is "not," that will help the team stay within scope, include it here.

- **Connect this work to other work, if applicable.** This comes in handy in two ways. First, sometimes you write an SOW for the first part of a project because this is all you can reasonably scope. Second, as a project grows, you may end up writing multiple SOWs—this helps tell the story of how they connect.

Here are a couple of examples from Hartke Designs SOWs.

Short and simple

Company X is looking for a partner to analyze their current management curriculum and redesign elements of the existing content to align with the new vision. In addition, they may identify new learning elements that need to be designed and developed as part of this initiative. For example, a new curriculum focused on "managers of managers."

More complex

Company Y is setting out to create an online learning curriculum focused on product training for five product lines: Paper, Ink, Printers, Scanners, and Shredders. The internal team has identified that they want to create a series of 10-15 eLearning modules for each product line.

Currently, Company Y has job role training that covers many of the products, but, as we understand it, that training is classroom based, and is too in-depth for all employees. However, to *not* provide any product training to certain audiences (e.g., new sales associates, remote workers, customer service, and support departments) is leaving a gap.

We will work alongside key stakeholders to articulate project specifics, create a strategy, and present a recommended way forward to design and develop this curriculum.

In this first engagement, we will immerse just far enough to create a high-level design for the overall curriculum. We will identify all courses, suggest how the topics might be chunked, make instructional design and development recommendations, and provide a detailed budget and timeline for the next phase of work.

Scope and deliverables

What it is: In my SOWs, this is a list of bullet points that lay out the work we are going to do and what we are going to deliver. Like the project summary, I go over this list in both team and client kickoffs to make sure that everyone working on the project, understands and agrees to the parameters.

The bulleted list is usually preceded by a statement like this, "The budget and timeline below assume the following design and development elements."

Why it matters: This is the meat and potatoes of the SOW. It is where you:

- State quantifiers that help define the edge of the scope sandbox. For example, in my SOWs for the design and development of training materials, I might include the:
  - Number of pages or screens we assume the content will include— e.g., "up to 30 screens"
  - Total learner seat time—e.g., "An up to 40-minute learning experience"
  - Total number of images, activities, and original graphics we plan to incorporate
  - Number of review cycles
- State technical requirements, if applicable. For example, in my business, I consider:
  - What tool (and version) we are using to build eLearning courses
  - What assumptions I am making about the client's technical environment (e.g., platform, browsers, devices, limitations around streaming video sizes)
- State functional specs, if applicable. For example, when my team and I build eLearning courses, we state:
  - What kind of audio narration we plan to use in the course and how many unique voices we plan to use
  - Whether we are building a graded assessment
  - Whether bookmarking will be used (meaning, the course remembers where a learner left off when they leave and re-enter a course)
- Define deliverables and your process. In my SOWs, this tends to be the same sub-section of the *Scope and deliverables* section. These are

literally the documents, files, print collateral, etc. that you are going to hand the client as you complete the project. In this section, you should:

- Name the deliverable
- Describe what it is
- Identify the technology you are going to use to create the deliverable

This is an example of how I describe the design document deliverable in my SOWs.

Design Document: An articulation of what learners will know and be able to do after completing the course. It provides a high-level content outline, wireframes for each of the screen types, and a global graphic design treatment. Delivered in Word. Clients are typically given one opportunity to review and feedback given on this deliverable are reflected in the next deliverable.

Things to consider:
- Use "up to..." language so that you can identify when scope creep is happening and to what degree it is happening, so that you are not bound to hit that number, and to avoid conversations about giving money back if you don't hit that number.
- If the section gets lengthy, consider using sub-headers to break up walls of text.
- Keep each bullet clear and crisp.
- Share this section with everyone on the team and make sure the project manager refers back to this anytime they are worried that the

scope might be creeping beyond the bounds of the original agreement.

Assumptions

What it is: In my SOWs, this is a two-part section that states clearly what Hartke Designs will do and what the client will do. It usually starts with this language, "In the interest of defining clear, achievable objectives and a shared vision for this project, please note that this proposal and cost estimate make the assumptions listed below."

Why it matters: This is a key part of any agreement as it's the section that you can clearly define how you will work, what you need from the client in order for the project to be successful, any assumptions about what the client will provide, what you will provide, and how you will handle specific situations should they arise.

Things to consider:

- Use clear, crisp, and plain language.
- Be comprehensive. Anything that you anticipate might be a gotcha as the project unfolds should have an assumption or two tied to it in this section.

Here are some sample assumptions that show up in my SOWs, depending on the project. Every SOW I write has an assumptions section, and the list tends to be longer on fixed bid projects (see the end of this chapter for an explanation of fixed-bid projects).

Hartke Designs will:

- Conduct the majority of this work at its own place of business, conferring with project team by phone, email, and occasional site visits as needed

- Provide a weekly written status report that documents key decisions, highlights upcoming important dates, flags risks, clearly outlines action items for all members of the team
- Hire up to four professional voice over actors and bill Company X as a direct expense for each talent after client has signed off on audio clips
- Not be available on these dates: [insert dates]
- Be available to begin work on [insert date]

Company X will:

- Assign a representative to the project who will grant all approvals, schedule meetings, provide information, and otherwise be availability to consult with Hartke Designs as required to complete this project.
- Provide source content and existing classroom materials at or before the kickoff meeting
- Limit their review of content materials to up to five people
- Consolidate all feedback from their reviewers and deliver one set of feedback that is free of contradictions
- Provide feedback within five business days of receiving each deliverable
- Not require translation
- Not deliver this course on mobile devices
- Complete all testing on their LMS and provide an issues log based on the results

Timeline

What it is: This is an articulation of the dates you plan to complete this work or the number of days or weeks you anticipate the work taking.

Why it matters: After wondering how much a project is going to cost, clients are most interested in how long it's going to take. And having a clear picture of how long a project is going to take will allow you to build a realistic budget.

Things to consider:

- Beyond providing a range of days or weeks, you might include a high-level project plan or timeline if the client asks for this or if it's a complex project with multiple moving parts.

- Include an end date. This could be stated as an exact date or a range of weeks of total duration that begins when the project kicks off. This is important if the project starts to elongate beyond what you can reasonably accommodate. Having this language will make it easier for you to talk about an exit strategy or a way to end the project, if needed.

This is an example of how I articulate a high-level timeline for a fixed bid project.

This project can be completed in 10-12 weeks. The duration is based on subject matter expert availability and ability to turn deliverable reviews around in three business days. Increased calendar time can have an impact on fixed-bid pricing.

Budget and payment terms

What it is: The bottom line and the first page your clients will flip to when they receive your proposal. This section can be as simple as stating the number of hours and the hourly rate. Or a table that expresses pricing for different deliverables, phases, or parts of the project.

Why it matters: Ahem. Duh!

Things to consider:

- Include when you plan to invoice. For example, I invoice monthly on the last day of the month. See the Steady Paycheck section in Chapter 2 for information on what to consider when it comes to your invoicing rhythms

- Up to how many days you anticipate it will take them to pay you— Expressed as "Net #" (e.g., Net 30, Net 60, etc.)

- If you anticipate doing any travel on the project, you should include any assumptions you are making about what expenses the client will cover, what information you will provide when you invoice, and when you plan to provide these invoices (e.g., invoiced within a week after your travel concludes). For example:
  - I include language that says I will not book travel without written permission.
  - I also include requirements for flying first class or business class for international travel.

For each contract you will have to decide whether to work on an hourly contract or a fixed bid contract. Some independents only work on an hourly basis. Others only work on a fixed-bid (or sometimes called "fixed-cost" or "fixed-price"). I tell prospects that I am happy to structure our contract either way, but prefer to work hourly unless the project is very well scoped. It is difficult to thoroughly define the edges of the scope sandbox if you don't really know much about the project.

If you have a client who insists on only working on a fixed bid, then split the project into phases and begin with a discovery phase. Then, make the deliverable of that phase a design document of some sort that defines the work for the next phase.

Contact information

What it is: The contact information for whomever in your company—probably you—that the client organization should contact. This section starts with this language in my SOW, "Please refer any questions or correspondence to."

Why it matters: In larger client organizations, it is possible that your business-side client will hand your SOW off to their purchasing department and you will work with someone in that department to execute the agreement. Having this information in the proposal is useful for them.

Things to consider:
- Include: Company name, contact name, mailing address, email address, and phone number

Project acceptance

What it is: A closing statement that basically asks that the client sign if the statement of work accurately reflects the agreement.
Why it matters: Again, duh.

Things to consider:

- Work with your attorney for the right language for this section.

- Include lines for your signature and the client's signature and date. Your attorney might want you to include more.

- It is possible that when you submit an SOW, the client will take language from your SOW and "put it on their paper." Meaning, they will put it into their standard contract document. If this happens, make sure they did not remove anything that is important to you and that they did not add something that you do not agree with. I've had many purchasing departments remove my assumptions section—which does not work for me. When this happens, I ask them to work it into the agreement or add it as a schedule at the end of the document. Consider having your attorney review the contract when it gets put on the client's paper.

Setting your rates

If you're just starting out, you are likely wondering how to set your rates. There are a couple approaches you can take.

Start with what a salaried person makes

In this approach, you take your current full-time annual salary (or the full-time salary of a person who does what you want to do), add whatever amount you'll have to pay for insurance, add whatever you estimate your business expenses might be (e.g., accountant, office space, office supplies, etc.) and divide that number by how many hours you think you'll work in a year. I suggest using 1,536 billable hours. This assumes 32 billable hours a week for 48 weeks. This allows some time each week for non-billable administrative tasks, sales, networking, and professional development. It also assumes you'll be taking about four weeks of vacation. Obviously push those numbers up or down based on your own work/life balance sensibilities.

If a salaried person makes $100,000 a year before benefits, you know you will pay $6,000/annually for insurance, you estimate you'll spend $2,000 for your accountant, and you estimate you'll spend $2,000 for postage/office supplies. That equals a total of $110,000. Divide that by billable hours (1,536). That equals $72/hour.

In my book, that is the least amount you should bill. However, the next thing to consider is what the market is actually paying. This leads me to the next approach.

What are other consultants who do what you do making?
It is well worth the possibly uncomfortable conversation where you ask someone else about their rates. If you have very trusted colleagues who are already independents in your field, then they will likely be happy to just flat out share their rates.

If you don't have close colleagues who are also independents, but rather have some acquaintances, you can approach it like this, "I understand you might not be comfortable sharing your exact rates, but can I share with you what I am thinking of charging and can you tell me if I should move up or down?" When I've done this, I've found people were honest about where I should and can reasonably position myself.

You can also ask trusted colleagues who are on the client's side and who hire people who do what you do. You can ask them, without naming names, "What sort of ranges are you seeing for independent consultants who do X."

Charge what you are worth and don't feel bad about it! ~ Sid, 30, freelance writer and communications specialist, Auckland, New Zealand

One thing that surprised me as I got started was how unwilling some potential clients are to pay a decent hourly rate, commensurate with years of expertise. I have to remind those people that freelancers need to cover their own benefits. And if they are not willing to pay what I need to make, I respectfully decline the work. ~ Greg, 58, talent development consultant, New York, NY

I was surprised by the amount of time it takes to actually get the first check on a project. From negotiations, contract signing, departmental signing on check requests, etc. It can take a while. Make sure you really understand the client's process. ~ Kelly, 70, consumer goods industry consultant, Chicago, IL

A Final
Word

I've loved (almost) every minute I've spent as an independent consultant. I love the fact that I get to choose the fabulous people I work with, that I get to pick my projects, and I can structure my time—which is absolutely finite and is the greatest gift we have—in a way that serves my goals and priorities.

And the reality is that this life is not for everyone. I applaud you for thinking deeply about whether this way of working is a fit for you. And there is absolutely no shame in discovering that the life of the independent consultant is not for you.

No matter what choice you make for yourself today or tomorrow, I wish you abundance and serenity as you walk through the rest of your days!

And, if this book helped you in some way that you want to share or there is a question you think my next edition should answer that is not covered here, please drop me a line!

Until then,

Gretchen

Chicago, IL
gigeconomy@hartkedesigns.com

Acknowledgements

Over the last ten years, thirty-five companies have trusted me and my team of thirty fellow independent consultants to bring their projects to life. It is because these human beings—both my clients and my colleagues—said yes, that I've had and continue to have the great honor to live this amazing life in the gig economy. It is no exaggeration to say that without them, I would be nowhere.

My deep gratitude goes out to Cara Lockwood, my friend and editor, who very early on encouraged me to keep writing. And then helped to shape every sentence and thought into something that makes sense outside of my head. Many thanks to Eric Hartke, my friend-for-life and go-to graphic designer. You make everything that Hartke Designs puts out into the world, including this book, look beautiful. And to Janet Russell for reading with eagle eyes to make sure my language was clear, concise, and correct.

In addition to the people who helped to bring this book to life, there are many people who feed my soul and keep me focused on the right things. My urban tribe makes sure that while I work alone most days, there is no day that I am actually alone. I send my love and light to Gretchen (the other one), Hillary, Dani, Beth, Cara, Julie, Annie, Kat, Heather, Sarah, Tanya, Mikki, Michelle G., Sandy, Michele E., Ryan, Trena, Stacey, Cathy MM, Ed, Bridget, Alissa, Pamay, Cate, and Tina.

And to my family who created the foundation on which I've built my personal and professional life. My Mom modeled the importance of being connected to the people around us. She doesn't know a stranger and her example made me the authentic networker I am today. My Dad showed me early in life what it looked like to be an entrepreneur —before I even knew that was a thing. I learned from him that the early bird gets the worm. And, my sister, who was my first friend and the person I count on to cheer me on and to tell me the truth no matter what.

Finally, to the two guys that give me a soft place to land. Tim, my partner, and love. And, Ocho, my fur baby. You both make the hard days easier and the great days spectacular.

Made in the USA
Lexington, KY
29 January 2019